Charles May

The Pioneers of Nashville and of Tennessee

A Historical Novel of Narrative, about the First Settlers of this Commonwealth of

1780 - Vol. 1

Charles May

The Pioneers of Nashville and of Tennessee
A Historical Novel of Narrative, about the First Settlers of this Commonwealth of 1780 - Vol. 1

ISBN/EAN: 9783337125875

Printed in Europe, USA, Canada, Australia, Japan

Cover: Foto ©ninafisch / pixelio.de

More available books at **www.hansebooks.com**

1780. 1880.

THE
Pioneers of Nashville,
AND OF TENNESSEE!
WHO THEY WERE!
WHERE THEY CAME FROM!
HOW THEY GOT HERE!
WHAT THEY ACHIEVED!
ONE HUNDRED YEARS AGO!

"HONOR TO WHOM HONOR IS DUE."

A Historical Novel of Narrative, about the first Settlers
of this Commonwealth in 1780.

TO WHICH IS ADDED:

An Historical Sketch about Robertson's and Donaldson's Ex
ploits and Adventures in the Foundation
on the Cumberland.

A Contribution to the Celebration of our Centennial
In 1880.

By CHAS. MAY.

Nashville American Print.

INTRODUCTION.

In this our Centennial year the history of the first Settlers becomes of necessity, a theme of recollection and veneration. We offer these few pages as a little contribution with that intention.

The pluck, achievements and struggles of our Forefathers are full of intense interest to us. By their valor and virtue they deserve to be held up to the wondering gaze and admiration of their descendants, and all who are now benefitted by their institution.

We owe them a debt of gratitude for their labors and perseverance.

This is the Hundreth Anniversary of the laying of the corner-stone of Nashville, Robertson and Donaldson meeting on the 24th of April, 1780. Indissolubly connected with the history of its Capitol is the history of the State.

What immense changes have taken place these hundred years! It now does not take as many *days* to travel through the whole length of the State as it took our Founders *months* to get from Watauga to the Bluff!

We refer the kind reader for a complete history of the subject to Haywood, Bancroft and Martin, but especially to Ramsey's Annals of Tennessee, from which these pages were partly copied and condensed.

We do not pretend to give a full history of Nashville, since that would take a volume; but in the words of Ramsey, "leave that duty to some admiring and grateful citizen of Nashville."

The first part of this pamphlet is a historical drama or novelette on the subject, partly fiction, partly matters of fact.

The second part, a short sketch of the history of Nashville, offers ample proof that the lives of these Pioneers were thoroughly full of exciting romance and adventure.

CHARACTERS.

COL. ROBERTSON, *Founder of Nashville.*
COL. DONALDSON, *his Associate.*
JOHN DONALDSON, *the latter's Brother.*
MRS. ROBERTSON.
BESSIE, *their Daughter.*
MANSCO,
EATON.
WELLS.
WINTERS. } Settlers.
STUMP.
JENNINGS.
PAT QUIGLY.
JONATHAN, *a funny character.*
JOHN BULL, *a Henglishman.*
MONSIEUR CHARLEVILLE, *a French Trader.*
MRS. DUNHAM.
MARY, *her Daughter.*
A NEGRO MAN AND WOMAN.
MOYTOY, *a friendly Cherokee Chief.*
CHULLOCULLA, *a hostile Cherokee Chief,*
ATTACULLA, *his Brother.*
TOKA, *Chief of the Creek Indians.*
RAVEN, *another Creek Indian.*
BIG FOOT, *a funny Indian.*
A SQUAW WITH HER BOY.
SEVERAL OTHER LADIES AND CHILDREN.

PIONEERS OF NASHVILLE.

CHAPTER I.

1.

AT WATAUGA.

Country people standing and sitting around; children playing; men smoking; one on guard against the Indians; negro woman nursing baby; negro man cleaning rifle.

JONATHAN. Man approachin'! Wall, I'll be darn', if that's one of our men; he must be a stranger. (*Loud.*) Halt there! what's your flag? (*Here all jumped up.*)

ROBERTSON (*enters.*) Why, Jonathan, don't you know me any more? I am—

JON. Wall, I'll be darn', if it hain't Robertson comin' back from prospectin' for a new location for a settlement! Where did you leave your comrades? Where is Mansco? Did the redskins not take your scalps? how did you—(*shaking hands.*)

ROB. Hold on, ask me one at the time, and maybe I'll answer.

JON. Good, I'm satisfied with that.

(*Meanwhile settlers surround him, saying:*)

All. Welcome back to Watauga! How did your expedition turn out?

Eaton. Did you find a good place for another station?

Wells. How far did you get?

Winters. Why, it is six months since you started!

Jennings. Shake hands, old chum!

Rob. I'm now very tired, but to satisfy your curiosity, I'll sit down and tell you my adventures in very few words. (*Sits down.*)

The route, which we pursued, both going there and coming back, was by Cumberland Gap, and the Kentucky trace to Whitley's Station, on Dick's River; thence to Carpenter's Station, on the waters of Green River; thence to Robertson's Fork, on the north side of that stream; thence down the river to Pitman's Station; thence crossing over to Little Barren at Elk Lick; thence passing the Blue Spring over to Big Barren; thence up to Drake's Creek to Maple Swamp; thence to Red River at Kilgore's Station: thence to a creek which we named after Mansco, and from there to French Lick.

This journey was a long one—

Jon. There must have been a long time between drinks?—

(*Robertson turns around frowning.*)

Excuse me for not interrupting you sooner; your story was a dry one. Now I must ask you a question. Do you know what the Governor of South Carolina said to the Governor of North Carolina?

MANSCO. Get out with your foolishness!

ROB. We were often tired to death. But at last we reached a place in a rich country nearly clear of large trees, which formerly had been occupied by a French trader from Crozat's colony at New Orleans. His store was built on a mound, on the west side of Cumberland River, near what we now call French Lick Creek, about seventy yards from each stream. The place is deserted now. There is a high bluff on the river, and a hill near it commands the surrounding lands; it is easily defended against an enemy. The ground is mostly rich, and just the thing we want for planting corn and raising cattle.

JON. I wonder if that part of the country is also subject to the Governor of North Carolina, like ours here,—

MAN. (*runs after him.*) Will you hush?

ROB. After staying there a number of days and examining the surroundings; after resting for some time, we started for home again.

And now my friends, I think we have one of the finest places to form a new settlement. I propose that we start for there, this winter yet. (*They all become restless.*) Let us see if any of you will join our expedition? I will return the same way we came.

DONALDSON. Some of our men and most of our women cannot travel so far by land. It would kill them. So I propose that most of us go aboard of boats, which we will float down the river, at least as far as to the Muscle Shoals in the Tennessee River. There we may cross over land to French Lick.

ROB. Suppose you take your "good boat Adventure," and as many more boats as are necessary to carry you all; and you be the Captain?

ALL. Yes, yes, let him be the captain.

EAT. I and my family will go by land, it issafer,

JEN. My friends and I will join Donaldson on the boat; I like to row.

DON. By the way, how is Robertson's family?

JON. Bessie, you mean?

(*Donaldson wants to strike him.*)

Why do you hit me? Because I made love to her when you were gone? But here she comes. Now ask her!

(*Meanwhile the others talk together.*)

ROB. So let us go and get ready for the journey. (*They withdraw, except Don. and Bessie who holds his hand.*)

JON. So they all start? Ye think I'll be left? I'll be darned if I do. I believe I'll go and take care of Donaldson, so that Bess won't have to cry!

Exit.

BESSIE. How long a time it was that you were

away! And now are you scarcely back to me, you want to leave again? Oh, dear! Can it be, that you and I must part? Can't you give up your course by water, and join my father's band for love of me? Must it come to separation? Would that I had not seen this heartrending hour!

DON. No, Bessie, it would not do! I must not deprive my comrads of a leader. I am an experienced boatman to whom alone the course of the vessels can be confided. I have made such trips before, as you know.

BES. Dear me! I have a presentiment that some misfortune will happen that will separate us forever, and I will see thee no more. (*She cries.*)

DON. (*Embracing her.*) Fear not dearest, the darkest hour of all is just before the dawn. I feel it, that the Providence of God will bring us to meet again; will you then be my darling wife, after we are reunited?

BES. Yes, love, with all my heart.

DON. So keep this ring from me and wear it always. (*They kiss one another.*)

BES. Farewell, dearest.

DON. Good-bye, love.

JON. (*Had overheard this parting; now he comes forward and mocks them saying:* That kiss sounded like the noise that is heard if a cow has stepped in the mud and now pulls the hoof out again, etc., etc.

2.

THE EMIGRANTS START FROM WATAUGA.

Don. Now, my friends, it is time for us to enter this good boat "Adventure." May heaven protect us and lead us to our destination.

Rob. Good speed and take courage.

Don. As you proceed by the way of Kentucky to the Big Salt Lick on the Cumberland, come across with some of your men to the Muscles Shoals in Tennessee River over in Alabama, there to make such signs that we might know you had been there, and that it will be practicable for us to go across there by land.

Rob. We will do that. Let you be cautious, and no misfortune will befall you! (*One party goes to the boat and on board, the others go to the opposite side. Many weep at parting. Jonathan also went. They say:* Farewell, perhaps to meet no more; farewell, perhaps forever. *Parents embrace children, sons and daughters their fathers and mothers, husbands their wives. Good-bye. Hurrah!*)

After they are all departed, Jonathan is seen to come in once more, saying: O! I always thought I'd forget something, but I couldn't for the world remember what it was. But now I have it. Here it is. (*Goes back in the cabin and takes a bottle out. He starts with the others.*) *Exit.*

3.
IN THE WILDERNESS.

Indians around a Camp Fire.

SCOUT. (*Yelling.*) Halloo! Paleface coming this way, ten times ten (*showing all his fingers*) invade our hunting ground, to break our wigwam, to steal our squaw and to kill our pappoose. Will our Indian brothers let them do that? Will we fight and kill pale face?

CHULLOCULLA (*gets up.*) Cherokee hear scout. Indians not let white men come. Up, warriors, victory or death!

WARRIORS. Much good! Me kill stranger!

(*They start in single file, cautiously.*)

CH. Hide yourselves behind trees in ambush.

After some time our emigrants (over land) came along. As soon as they are all in sight, (Bessie and a little boy in the rear) Indians fire, yell a warhoop and rush upon them. Much confusion ensues. Travelers gather and return the fire. Bessie and the boy are cut off from the party. Chulloculla and another Indian reach and capture them. She screams and struggles to get loose, but the savages carry them off. Some whites fall down dead or wounded, some Indians likewise; one of the latter scalps a man. Finally they escape in a hurry.

Meanwhile some whites run after the chief and Bessie, to her rescue. Travelers kill the disabled Indians. After that they look around if anybody is missing.

ROB. Where is my daughter Bessie?

MAN. She was in the rear of our train when I last saw her. She was tired and going lame.

EAT. I saw that Cherokee devil jumping upon her, knock her down and drag her away. I shot at him, but must have missed him.

ROB. What? for heaven's sake! can that be? Which way did they flee with her?

EAT. This way.

ROB. Up! Let us pursue the infernal rascals and not return till our bullets have reached those robbers!

(*The women nurse the wounded and weep over the dead.*)

MRS. ROB. Oh! what terrible misfortune has befallen us! Would to God, that we never had entered this wilderness! Woe to me, my child, my only child! Fallen into the hands of these brutes! Heaven, hear the prayer of a bereaved mother, and deliver my child from a lot which is worse than death!

LADY. Have confidence in God, my dear. It is not yet all lost. Our men have gone to her rescue. After some time R. and the others came back.

Mrs. Rob.   O, where is my daughter?

Rob.   It was impossible to follow them. They retreated over yonder stony bluff, where we could see no trace whatever. Our torches gave out. We must give up pursuit now, before we are attacked again by some other band of redskins. After we have arrived at our destination and the women and children are in safety, we will come back here to exterminate them.

Mrs. Rob.   O God, O God! help my unfortunate child!

Jon, *who had hid himself in a thicket when the Indians came, now crawls out, and looks around cautiously. When he sees that there is no more danger, takes out his bottle and gives the wounded to drink, saying:*   Didn't the Governor say, there was a long time * * * *   *At last he knocks the bottle to pieces over the head of one of the dead Indians.*

4.

ARRIVAL AT THE FORT.

Settlers sitting around.

Wells.   So we are here now, at last, and safe.

Eat.   Thanks be to God. This was an awful march, ninety day's journey in the wilderness, over mountains, hills and rocks, through swamps, rivers and weeds, traveling all day and having no rest at night for fear of the Indians. And such rough weather and such an intense cold, as our oldest men do not recollect. All the rivers frozen over, and ever so deep a snow lying on the ground now as long as we were on our way! But this is no wonder as we have Mr. Winter (*turning to the gentleman of that name*) with us all the way.

W̱ɪɴ. You may well jest now, since we have built this fine log house and ever so warm a fire in it. But we must soon leave all this comfort again to fight the Indians, who have captured Bessie Robertson.

Sᴇᴛ. I wonder if Col. Donaldson and his crew are alive yet, as it seems they never will come?

Eᴀᴛ. I was away down the river to-day, but have seen and heard nothing of them. I believe now we must give them up for lost!

Wᴇʟ. No, no! Do not speak such terrible words! I hope and pray, Almighty God will protect our wives and children and kinfolks on the boats.

Wɪɴ. I have a presentiment that will we hear of them soon. I will go down the river once more; but if my inspiration is not verified this time, I will believe in presentiments no longer.

Sᴇᴛ. They must suffer terribly from exposure to snow and cold, and to the bullets and arrows of the savages. (*A shot is heard in the distance.*)

Eᴀᴛ. Hark! What was that? A cannon shot?

(*Another shot is heard nearer.*) Another? That's nothing else than Donaldson and his crew! (*They start up.*)

The boat "*Adventure*" is seen rowing up. They meet the crew, who jump out, embrace each one of their families; they laugh and weep for joy alternately. Some shout: The good boat "Adventure." others: welcome,—greeting,—hurrah,—good luck. Well done—welcome to French Lick our new home—hurrah for the heroes!

(*Jonathan greets them with his bottle.*)

They march up, (*fife and drum ahead,*) in procession, all jubilant, singing "*Sweet Bye and Bye*," etc.

JON. 'Haint that like the ship "Pinafore?"

5.

NARRATIVE OF THE "ADVENTURE."

(*Don. stands up; the others sitting around.*)

ROB. Now, as your struggles are over, do tell us your adventures up and down the rivers.

DON. Took our departure from the Fort at Watauga, Dec. 22, last year, and fell down the river to the mouth of Reedy Creek. The frost was most excessively hard, as you recollect. One day we had lost Harrison, who had gone a hunting. After firing many guns to fetch him in, we found him again the third day. Capt. Hutchin's nigger died, having frosted his feet and legs. E. Peyton's wife was delivered of a child. Indians invited us to a village where they massacred poor Stuart, his family and friends, 28 in number, who had to be singled off in the rear, because they were afflicted with smallpox. We heard their pitiful cries. Again a boat sank, and as we bailed her, the Indians nearly ruined our whole expedition, firing on us in great numbers from a bluff above us.

JON. Here I come in without leave, and that's what I always say, there is a long time—

(*Cries: Spank him, take him out!*

DON. So we came down Holston and Tennessee rivers. We had lost Jennings' boat, perhaps to be slaughtered by the merciless enemy, but next day he came up to us, after having lost his nigger, all his cargo and a man; his boat, his and his wife's clothes being riddled by the Indian's bullets.

At the Muscles Shoals we vainly looked for the marks that you had promised to put there, to invite us to cross over on the land. The waters roared terribly, and driftwood was heaped around. The currents ran in all directions. Here we did not know how soon we would be dashed to pieces, and all our troubles ended at once. We knew not the length of the shoal; they say it is 25 or 30 miles, but we passed it in three hours.

JEN. The 20th of February, we arrived at

the mouth of the Tennessee. Our situation was desperate. We were worn down by hunger and fatigue, the current was rapid, our boats not constructed to stand a strong current, and now we had to row up the stream. We knew not the distance we had to go, nor how much longer it would take us. Several boats would not proceed with us, but were bent to Mississippi or Illinois. They part, perhaps to see us no more. Happen what will, we were determined to pursue our course.

DON. Friday, 24th, we came to the mouth of a river, which we took to be the Cumberland, but were not certain. Some said it could not be it. It was so much smaller than we expected. We ventured to make the trial. We suffered much from hunger and fatigue. Next day we knew it was the Cumberland. Killed a swan and some buffalo. Gathered some herbs. Friday 31st, we met Col. Henderson, who was running the line between Virginia and North Carolina.

JON. That's my place, and here is to the Governor!

DON. He gave us all information and promised us some seed corn. Now we are here.

ALL. Hail ye heroes, heavenborn band! Hurrah!

CHAPTER II.

I.

AT THE BLUFF.

(Mrs. Rob. and Don. standing, the rest sitting.)

DON. I almost forgot! Where's Bessie?

MRS. ROB. We have lost her!

DON. What? lost her? how? where?

MRS. ROB. A frightful misfortune has befallen us! I cannot tell you. Grief almost breaks my heart!

DON. Oh! woe to me! How can it be? *(crying.)* She had a presentiment when we started that she would not see me any more. Alas! that it should be verified so soon! But how was it?

MRS. ROB. It was March 3d, early in the morning, when the Cherokees, who had laid in ambush, surprised us, firing from all bushes, killing and scalping six of our men. Bessie then was a little in the rear, when three of the red devils captured her. It was heartrenting to hear her cries.

(Ladies Weep.)

DON. God damn the red skins! Have you no news what became of her? They didn't kill her?

Mrs. Rob. No, but what is worse than death, Chulloculla, the chief, wants to make her his squaw. The boy whom they robbed with her, escaped them and reached us.

Don. Death and hell upon these Cherokees! Rise, comrades, up and against them! May this, my right arm wither if I rest before I have dispatched them to the infernal regions!

Mrs. Rob. My husband went back in search of her. As he alone was powerless against the whole band, he took a great many articles for presents with him which the Indians like, such as rifles, knives, blankets and whisky.

Jon. There he done me a great wrong in taking that from me, and to the Governor of North Carolina too.

(*One of the men strikes him.*)

Don. Have you no news from him?

Mrs. Rob. Yes, sir! A friendly Creek Indian brought us this letter from him.

Don. Who is the carrier? I want to see him.

(*Big Foot Indian comes in.*)

Don. Are you the Creek Indian?

Big F. Me be a Creek Indian.

Don. What is your name?

B. F. Big Foot, the Cherokee Killer.

Don. Who gave you that name?

B. F. Every one that know me.

Don. How many Cherokees did you kill already?

B. F. Me—me—Cherokee tremble, me come.

Don. I don't think you deserve that name then.

B. F. See rifle, bow and arrows, spear and tomahawk. Bear see me and fly. Even Massa Rob. call me so.

Don. Tell me something about Robertson.

B. F. Me been at Quorina, where I led a band of Chickasaw Indians to Drake's Creek. You know, me be great leader of Indians.

Don. Do you tell the truth, Big Foot?

B. F. (*Proudly.*) Me tell no lie—except—I must.

Don. That I believe. Now tell me through which settlements and Indian villages must we pass?

B. F. Kilgrove Station to Red River, Maple Swamp, Drake's Creek.

Don. How long will it take us to get there?

B. F. That many suns. (*Holds up three fingers.*)

Don. I suppose you are right. Now tell me where Robertson is?

B. F. Massa Robertson find me at Drake's Creek. He be my brother, give me much present and that letter, send me here to tell you where Bessie be.

Don. Where can I meet him?

B. F. Near a big rock on the creek.

(*Raven, a Cherokee, comes in boldly, looks around saying nothing. Big Foot stands back.*)

Mrs. Rob. Speak to him Don.; he is the Cherokee, who came here regarding Bessie.

Raven. How d'ye!

Don. (*Short.*) How d'ye!

R. You not be my man.

Don. You have no business with any other!

R. Me no come to see *you!*

Don. Then you better go out!

R. (*Turns around to go; so does Don. Raven comes back, says:* Sirrha! (*Don. goes on.*)

R. (*Louder*) Sirrha!

Don. (*Turns his head only:*) What else?

R. Me speake to you.

Don. Then be polite, or I'll throw you out. What is your name?

R. Me be Raven, Cherokee nation.

Don. Who sent you here?

R. Chulloculla, great chief of Cherokee.

Don. Was he the chief who captured Bessie?

R. It was he.

Don. Why does he not give her free? has he not received a ransom twice already?

R. Chief has many warriors, all want rifles, knives, blankets and firewater.

Jon. That's what I want, too; this is what the Governor of South Carolina meant—

Man. Knock that fool down!

Don. Your chief is a liar and a thief, his tongue is

double like the serpent's. You will get no ransom any more.

R. Then Betsie will be squaw of chief or die.

DON. He will not give her up this time either although we send him ransom again,

R. Chief be good, let Betsie go.

DON. Do you speak the truth? Swear by the Great Spirit!

R. M—e—e no swear.

DON. Then you are a liar and a thief!

R. (*Draws his knife.*) You pale face son of a bitch!

DON. (*Knocked him down.*) Down, Indian dog!
(*Mrs. Rob. and ladies shrieking.*)

DON. Tie his hands and feet and keep him captive.

(*Pat Quigley comes in; takes a hold of Raven.*)

PAT. Faith an' be jabers, hand him to me! It is the likes of me that can clinch him!

DON. Oh! there is Pat; welcome here on the Bluff.

PAT. I hear you going to rescue Bessie; kin I go along?

DON. Certainly, Pat; I'm glad if you do.

PAT. Does this Indian with his armory go with us?

DON. Yes, sir! He will be our guide.

PAT. Hurrah! I likes him! Begoorah, I'm

gleed that I kin go to fight ag'in. (*Leaps and dances for joy.*)

JON. Pat, lets you and me go in partnership; suppose you be Governor of South Carolina, etc., etc. (*They all start to go.*)

Exeunt.

2.

AT AN INDIAN CAMP.

Chulloculla and Bessie.

CH. (*Chulloculla drags Bessie in by the hand; she struggles against it.*) Now white squaw be in my power!

BES. ·I know it, miserable wretch; you have robbed me from my father and mother. How would you feel if the whites had captured your daughter? Let me go back then, otherwise their warriors will come and kill you to make me free.

CH. Me no will. You must be my squaw!

BES. (*Scornfully.*) No, never, never! you rascal, you thief, you murderer! (*Jumps at him.*)

CH. (*Throws her down; she falls on her knees.*) Be quiet or me kill you!

BES. Rather die than be the wife of an Indian hound. Let me alone!

CH. Come and be my squaw, otherwise I will force you to be my slave. (*Hugs her.*)

BES. (*Shrieks.*) Help, help! (*Tries to escape.*)
CH. There be nobody to help you. (*Laughing.*) Will you be my mistress and have all my other squaws for your slaves, all my ponies to ride on, all my trinkets that I robbed from white man for your own, and my heart, (*kneels down before her*) for your love?

BES. No, no, a thousand times no! Do you see this ring! My heart and hand are engaged to a white chief. (*Snatches his knife from him; tries to stab him.*) Die from my hand, as my heart despises you! (*He catches up her arm and takes knife from her. He gets up. She scratches and beats him, and bites him in the arm, when he holds her hands tight, she kicks him.*)

BES. God Almighty come to my assistance against this devil. (*Shrieks.*) Help, help!

ATTACULLA. (*Comes in.*) She no want to be squaw of chief? She want to be *my* squaw then. (*Interferes, holds her down.*) Me be brother to Chulloculla.

BES. What? You infernal scoundrel! (*Spits in his face.*) Begone!

SCOUT. (*Comes in a hurry; shouts:* Creek warriors coming, catch your ponies! Our braves meet them!

(*Chulloculla binds her hands together and drags her in the fort. Returns.*)

Up, warriors! Upon them! *Exeunt.*

3.

AT A TRADING STATION.

A Trader, his Wife and a Negro seated.
(Enters Don. and party.)

DON. Good evening, friends! Can we stay here over night and have something to eat? We are coming from French Lick to-day, and are very tired.

JON. I'm in for something to drink, rather

CHARLEVILLE. (*Getting up,*) You gome from le Bluff? Welcome! Dot's de blace I used to sday. Mahree, go to make subber for dem. I guess you go back to Watauga?

DON. No, Monseur! We go to Drake's Creek to punish the Cherokees for robbing Bessie Robertson from our train.

CHARL. Dot's right; kill dem all. As for me, I am a trader, an' canno' shoot. I have some gattle and ship (*sheep*) here, but dere is a pear (*bear*) in de neighborhood, dot I canno gheep (*keep*) from stealing my ship.

DON. I have a talisman against all beasts of prey.

CHARL. What is it?

DON. (*Takes rifle and aims at him.*) This is it

CHARL. (*Fleeing.*) For God's saghe, flee, he is insane!

DON. No sir! I'm not insane, but you are a coward. Show me your sheep-pen!

CH. Bag (*back*) here. The bear ghills (*kills*) an' eats a ship every night. (*D. turns to go.*)

JON. Stay here, or the bear will eat you too, and have nothing except your boots?

DON. If he should eat you, he'd leave nothing except your whisky bottle.

PAT. Let me go with ye, it is the likes of me, as kin kill beers.

DON. No, Pat; you are no hunter and would only expose our lives and be in my way.

(*Pat. wants to go with them, but Don. keeps him back. Donaldson takes rifle; it is dark; men go in cabin. Don. steps on tiptoe, hides himself and waits. After a while the bear is heard grunting. Comes up close where Don. is. He shoots, and bear rolls on the ground howling. Another bear is heard in the distance, coming up. Don. scarcely has time to load his gun, when the bear hugs him. He draws his knife and kills him after a wrestle. He goes back to cabin. Men come out, not seeing bears.*)

JON. You've done a good thing, you've scared the bear, that he won't come to-night to eat sheep.

DON. But Mrs. Bear has come and her husband too. But now they are lying side by side.

CHARL. Do you spick (*speak*) the droot? (*truth*).

DON. Look here, Jon. My boots are not hurt. My talisman has worked wonders. Now, take the skins.

PAT. Faith and bigorrah, what a baste! (*beast*) me rifle would have shaked!

JON. (*Jon. and Pat. quarrel for the skins.*) Give it to me!

PAT. The likes of me as shall have it!

JON. My boss killed the bear, I was with him.

PAT. Be jabers, you shan't. (*They both pull hard, at last both fall to the ground.*)

B. F. There are the tow governors, one from South Carolina and the other from North Carolina

4.

IN THE WILDERNESS.

The Duel.

(*Don. espies tracks on the ground, follows them and discovers Toka; he stops him crying*; Halt, red man; *Toka looks around.*)

DON. Will red man be pale face's brother?

TOKA. What be your name?

DON. Donaldson, and we come from French Bluff.

TOKA. Are you brother to Robertson?

DON. Yes, I am! Have you seen him?

TOKA. Me seen him. Rob sent me to you.

Don. Where is he at?

Toka. He be by Drake's Creek, he make marks there for his white brother.

Don. Then thanks be to the Great Spirit that I saw your track, otherwise you would have missed me.

Toka. Toka find white brother any way; me want drink water, me come back to buffalo path, see your track there and follow you to see if brother or no.

Don. What's your name?

Toka. Me have no name. Me name be buried under ground of my wigman, till me fulfill which me have sworn by the Great Spirit; call me Toka, father without sons.

Don. Have they killed your sons?

Toka. That muchee sons (*holding up 3 fingers*), as high as tree, brave as chiefs. Me find them dead and scalped.

Don. Who has killed them

Toka. Chulloculla, Cherokee Chief. He steal my ponies to carry his robbers, my skins to make them mocasins. But me rifle has killed so much (*showing three fingers*) of his warriors, my arrow so much (*four fingers*) and my knife so much (*six fingers*). But the devil is with him that my eye could not see him and my hand not get him. But he will go to hell anyway, you and Robertson hold together. Bullet of Robertson never missee. Cherokee fear him. He come and go but be invisible. Hear his rifle and tremble. Warrior no catch him.

DON. How far is it yet to Drake's Creek?

TOKA. That muchee suns (2 *fingers*). (*Here they meet the others again. Don. turns to them.*)

DON. This is Toka, a Creek brave, our scout now.

B. F. (*Angrily*). What? he know better than me?

TOKA. (*Looks at B. F. scornfully*). You be squaw!

B. F. Me kill so much bear. (2 *fingers*). Me will lead Massa, but you hang to tail of my pony.

TOKA. (*Wants to shoot him, others interfere.*) What be your name?

B. F. ·Greater than number of your fathers, and longer than your memory—Big Foot, the Cherokee Killer.

TOKA. You insult me. I have satisfaction. Me fight an Indian duel with you! Do as I do. (*He draws his knife, squats down, puts his knife to the calf of his leg and knocks it in with his fist.*) Me no kill squaw; do same as me.

B. F. Me have no time to squat down, me must go.

DON. We have plenty of time for a duel, to see, who is the bravest. Squat down too, and do the same as he does.

(*Big Foot squats down reluctantly and slowly,*

takes his knife trembling, grunts and moans, but does not stick it in. Pat comes behind him, and knocks it in with all his might. B. F. jumps up, yells terribly:) Be you mad? what be my leg for you? You louse, you flea, you groundhog, you pisscat!

PAT. Faith an' be jabers, the knife must come out again. (*pulls it out; B. F. howls loud, writhing with pain; falls down fainting. Others laugh heartily; one of them bandages his leg.*)

JON. (*Comes and gives him to drink, saying:*) Here is the Governor, as I always say.

5.

THEY MEET ATTACULLA.

The same.

TOKA. Here me see much tracks of horse.

DON. (*Coming up*) Sure enough; in this wilderness! They must be whites, for their horses were shod. They were going that way into the swamps.

TOKA. They cannot get through there. From what they have thrown away here, it is certain, that they are tired to death, otherwise they would not have dropped such valuable articles.

PAT. The train must have lost their way, bedad, I think they are of our paple.

TOKA. Me suppose, Indian get them in ambush.

DON. Hurry up then, that we may reach and warn them.

(*They haste and find a train of whites, led by an Englishman.*)

DON. Who is the leader of this train?

ANS. Give us to eat, we are starving, for all our ammunition is gone. (*They give them to eat.*) This Englishman is our leader. (*All gather around.*)

JOHN BULL. I am the leader. What do you want?

DON. Where are you coming from, and where going?

J. BULL. Must you know it?

DON. Have you reason, not to tell me?

J. B. (*Hesitating*) N-o, we are going to French Lick.

DON. Is that your direction? Your course leads east into the swamps, whereas Salt Lick lies west.

J. B. You are a liar, Fr. Lick is east.

DON. Look here, you scoundrel, if you give me the lie, I'll thrash you like a spaniel.

J. B. (*Wants to shoot him, others check him.*) Go to hell!

TOKA (*aside to Don*) Me believe he be traitor, an agent of the English, and wants to lead this train in ambush to the Indian Cherokees, to rob and kill them, if they are nearly starved and out of powder.

(*Here two more Cherokees come, Attaculla and Raven, who had made good his escape from the Bluff. They do not see Don and his party at first.*)

ATTACULLA. Welcome, brothers; who is the leader of this train?

J. B. I am, my friend. We are going to French Lick.

ATTA. Well, me go there, me go along.

Raven (*sees Don.*] Do you know me?

DON. Yes, I know you; who is your companion?

ATTA. You struck this brave man? He was a messenger; you must die!

DON. He insulted me, and I punished him justly.

TOKA. (*Aside to Don.*) He is Attaculla, brother of Chulloculla.

ATTA. This train will be in French Lick to-morrow.

DON. No, it will not, this Englishman is a traitor, he leads you in a false direction and into the swamp, there the Cherokee will lay in ambush—

ATTA. You lie!

DON. I dare you to call me a liar, or—(*takes his knife; Big Foot and Jona. hide themselves.*)

ATTA. Serpent! Your tongue is poison! You lie! (*takes his rifle to shoot Don. but Don. had anticipated this, raises his pistol and shoots Atta.*)

DON. You are Chulloculla's brother; I'm Bessie's bridegroom. Go to hell and announce it to Satan, that your whole band will follow. (*Atta. falls down dead. Toka scalps him.*)

DON. Come here now friends, and let us judge

this man, John Bull. (*They surround him. Big Foot, who had hid himself; now comes up and posts himself before John Bull, saying:*) Look at me, speak the truth and tell me no lie, otherwise my tomahawk will eat you up, you murderer, you robber, you liar, you—you—

Don. You answer me now! Did you want to lead this train in an ambush?

J. B. I am a subject of King George, to whom this colony belongs, and I acknowledge no judge but him.

Don. You were going to take these men into death; blood for blood, your life is forfeited to us.

J. B. I was going with them to Big Salt Lick.

Don. I will shoot you on the spot (*holding the pistol in his face*) if you don't tell the truth! Where is Chulloculla and his warriors?

J. B. I—I—yonder, in the fort at Drake's Creek. He was to come to-night and rob the train.

Don. How many are there in his band?

J. B. They were all coming together.

Don. Is this the first train you drove into his hands?

J. B. I—I—I—

Don. I will pardon you if you deliver him to us.

Toka. (*Rushing forward.*) Me have swore to

kill all brothers of Chulloculla. (*Stabs him; he sinks down and dies.*)

DON. Will you follow me, friends, in going to trace up Chulloculla, and deliver Bessie?

ALL. Yes, we will! Up, let us go!

JON. (*Aside.*) Let them rip! While they are gone, I'll tell you my story of the two Governors:

"I am sixty years old, and never got drunk till day before yesterday," remarked old Uncle Jonathan, as he sat on a large tree lying flat on the ground. "I have lived in Arkansas for forty years—cum here from East Tennessy—and the thought that I got drunk in the evening of my life, when I can just see my gray hairs shining in twilight, is enough to make me throw myself into the river."

"Tell us how it occurred, Uncle Jonathan," said a bystander.

"Well, some time ago up in my neighborhood," and he stopped talking and drew his pipe vigorously to see if the fire was out, "a Good Templar's Lodge was organized. All the young people in the community jined, and pretty soon they came after me. My son Ike was the leadin' man, and says he to me, 'Pap, I want you to jine this thing.' 'Ike,' says I, 'I don't know the taste of liquor, and I don't see the use of jinin'.' 'Pap,' says he, 'we want your influence. We are gwine to vote on the Local Option Law pretty soon, and we want you publicly identified with the work.' Then my daughter, she came around and begged me to jine. 'Susan,' says I, 'you never seed your old father take a drink.' 'No, Pap, says she, 'but we want you to help us to frown down the curse of intemperance.' Next our parson came around and sot my wife on me, and when they all got to drummin' I had to jine. I jined on a Friday night, and on the following Saturday I got on the boat and come down here. Something ailed me. Something kept saying Jesse White you ain't a free man. It bothered me, and when I saw one of the deck-hands turn up a jug I wondered if he had ever taken the pledge, and when he set the jug down I walked around and looked at it, took hold of the corncob stopper, walked away and smelt my fingers. I went up on deck and set down in front. Pretty soon two men came out and set down. After awhile one of them remarked: 'The Governor of North Carolina said to the Governor of South Carolina,' and without finishing the sentence both men laughed and drank out of a big black bottle. Thar was something in that Governor business that took me. I had heard my father talk about it and laugh. ' I had often heard it, but no one had ever been positive what it was the Governor said, only that time between the drinks had been rather long. Pretty soon one of the men reached down, took up the bottle, took out the cork and said :

'The Governor of North Carolina said to the ——.' Then both men laughed and drank. I never felt so curious in my life. I looked around at the trees on the bank, and the women who waived their handkerchiefs at us as they passed. Those Governors had a ring about them that tingled through my old blood. Just then one of the men turned, held the bottle toward me, and said: 'The Governor of North ——.' Before I knew it I had hold of the bottle. I turned it up and drank. All I thought about was the Governors, and, when the shadows of Ike, Susan and the parson and my wife flitted through my brain, the two Governors, tall and grand, stalked right up and ran over them. 'The Governor of North Carolina,' and I had another pull, and a long one. I began to see the Governors in their true light. I thought they were the best fellows in the world. The boat seemed to be running a mile a minute, and I didn't care what she did, so long as the Governors were with us. Well, boys, the Governors kept a remarkin' and I kept pullin', and by the time I got to Little Rock I was as drunk as an owl. Oh, I was drunk as a mule—a mink. I got off the boat and yelled, 'Hoorah for the Governor of North Carolina!' and the first thing I knowed I found myself in a sort of a prison. First time I ever was locked up, boys. Fust time I ever was drunk, and am sixty odd years old."

6.

AT THE INDIAN FORT.

Indian on Guard.

INDIAN GUARD. Here I watch for our band, that pale face cannot steal Bessie, white squaw of chief; white brother of her sneak around.

DON. (*Approaching him, crawling on the ground.*)

GUARD. Stop! who be there?

DON. (*Rising.*) Where is Chulloculla?

G. (*Levelling his rifle.*) Say the pass-word!

DON. I am John Buil. Where is the chief?

G. He is not in the fort.

DON. (*The report of a gun is heard.*) Who is shooting?

G. Thàt be pale face, father to Bessie.

DON. What is he shooting?

G. He sneak around like fox to shoot guard; say your pass-word if you be John Bull.

DON. Here it is! (*stabbing him.*)

ROB. (*is heard in the distance.*) Hallo—ee—o—

DON. (*Answers him.*) Hallo—ee—o—. (*They meet and embrace one another.*)

DON. Welcome in the wilderness!

ROB. Quick, let us load rifles! (*Loading.*)

ROB. Are you alone?

DON. No, sir!. I have four men with me.

Rob. Where did you halt?

Don. Down here on the creek. Where is Bessie?

Rob. In the fort yet. Let us go back to our fellows.

7.

THE FORT TAKEN.

The fort is a loghouse, decorated with scalps, bows and arrows, etc.

(Don. and Rob. in the distance, crawling on the ground toward the fort. Their party concealed behind bushes and trees.)

Rob. Here is the fort, the headquarters of Chulloculla and Bessie's place of captivity.

Don. How can we get at it? If there is a strong garrison of Cherokees in it, it takes too many lives to take it by force. I'll tell you what I'll do. I'll pretend to be that "Britisher," John Bull and pass the guard, go in and take Bessie with me, thus making good our escape.

Rob. That won't do. You'll certainly be killed.

Don. I fear not. Something must be done before Chulloculla gets home.

Rob. Good. I'll go with you for guard.

(They come in front of fort.)

G. *(Comes out of the door.)* Stop, who be there?

Don. John Bull and his brother.

G. That be a· lie! down! (*Levels gun to shoot; gun snaps; Don. shoots him.*) Off with you! (*Rob. stays at the door, Don. enters, comes out with Bessie to make their escape. Warned by the shooting, the band of Indians, led by Chulloculla rush upon them, the latter shoots at Don. but misses him; the Indians raise the warwhoop, yelling terribly. A party of the whites rush forward and attack the Indians; the latter retreat, leaving Chulloculla and Don. in the foreground. Don draws his sword to defend himself against Chulloculla's strokes with his rifle. They fight for some time, Don. holding Bessie by the hand. The latter draws a knife, and just as Chulloculla is lifting up his gun for a mortal blow upon Don., she buries the knife in his bosom, while Rob. at the same time shoots him at a little distance. Chulloculla drops down dead. Yet Don. is dangerously wounded; he also sinks down, intercepted by Bessie's arms. He raises himself up again. The Indians have disappeared, leaving their dead and wounded. Whites triumphant shout. Victory! Hurrah for Bessie!*)

JON. This was a hard fight and a long time between drinks.

CHAPTER III.

I.

FORT AT THE BLUFF ATTACKED.

MRS. DUNHAM. (*Seen with a little girl carrying a water-pail coming out of the fort.*) Go now, my child and get some water from the spring.

GIRL. Oh, mother! I am so much afraid of the Indians who killed and scalped father the other day.

MRS. DUN. O, no dear! They won't hurt you; they never hurt little girls; they like them; we have had no water in three days.

G. Will you stay here and watch for me till I come back?

MRS. DUN. Yes, child, I will. Fear not!

(*Girl goes out. Indians have been watching, run up after her, throw her down and scalp her. As Mrs. Dun. sees this, she leaps to the child's rescue. They knock her down also and scalp her.*

INDIAN. (*Holding up scalp, yell and shout:*) Hurrah, another pale face scalp! We swear to rest no till we have all their scalps!

(*Mother and child are stunned, after a while get up and cry:*) O dear, dear! (*Child says:*) O mother,

mother! Red men have killed me! (*They run back in the fort. Settlers rush out of the fort, armed, to run after the Indians who flee; other Indians run in between the whites and the fort to cut them off from retreat. All shoot; one Indian is killed, also one of the settlers; another is wounded and scalped. The Indians leave him to pursue his comrades. Being stunned, he lies on the ground for time; after a while he recovers and looks around in great pain. Supposing the Indians had left, he gets up; the Indians see him, laugh at him and mock him. As he wanted to run away, the Indians overhaul him and knock him down with their tomahawks.*)

IND. (*Shout:*) Frenchman give us a prize for every scalp we give them. We will soon have them all!

The other men being left without ammunition had retreated and closed the doors.)

2.

A WAR COUNCIL.

On the Bluff.

(*Settlers sitting around, Rob. stands up.*)

ROB. We are here in council to see what we can do to prevent the Indians from attacking us constantly. (*Sits down. Mansco gets up.*)

MAN. Our situation here is endurable no longer.

We cannot plough for our corn this spring, nor do any work on our fields without having our men shot down every time they venture to go out. No day passes that some of us are not shot at by the Indians. They are all gathered together, Cherokees, Creeks and Chickasaws to completely destroy us. I have broken up my (Mansco) settlement already. Many of the terrified settlers moved to Kentucky, or down the river. I think we must give up here too and all move away.

EAT. The Indians burnt up everything at my (Eaton's) Station, immense quantities of corn and other produce, houses and fences. All who could get off did so and came to this fort; but many never saw their comrades again in those places; some were killed sleeping, others were awakened only to be apprised that their last moment was come. Death seems ready to embrace all of us adventurers. Two men who had slept a little longer than others, were shot by the Indians' guns pointed through a port-hole. It is strange that all of my fellows did not leave before the impending danger. I, for my part, would give it up in despair.

JON. So do I. We better go hang ourselves to give the Indians no more trouble.

MAN. A numerous body of Cherokee warriors came here in the night and lay armed in ambush. Nex morning three of them came in sight, and fired at our fort, withdrawing immediately. Nineteen horsemen in the fort at once mounted their horses, and followed them. When they came to the branch they discovered Indians in the creek and in the thickets near it. These arose from their places of concealment and fired upon the horsemen. The latter dismounted to give them battle, and returned their fire with great alacrity. Another party of the enemy lay concealed in the brush and cedars ready to rush in the fort, in rear of the combatants. The horses ran away—the men being left on foot. To guard the fort the gates were closed.

JON. So was my bottle, but now I open it again.

EAT. In the meantime the battle raged without. Five men were killed on the spot, among them Capt. Leiper. Others were wounded before they could reach the fort. Some Indians ran after the loose horses to capture them. This circumstance and our trained dogs broke their line, otherwise none of us would have reached the fort any more. The nine who survived would have had to break through the line, their own guns being empty, whilst those of the Indians were well charged.

JON. (*Aside.*) So was my bottle empty but I'm agoing to have it charged.

MAN. Now, therefore, all those who are in favor of breaking up this settlement and going off will rise up with me. (*All arise except Rob. and Don.*)

Rob. My friends, I am against this hasty step. For where could we go to ? It is impossible to reach Kentucky. The Indians are in force on all the roads and passages leading there. For the same reason it is impossible to reach the settlements on the Holston. No other means of escape remain but going down the river in boats to make good our retreat to the Illinois. But how is the wood for such boats to be obtained? The Indians are lying concealed day and night among the shrubs ready to kill any one who ventures to go out.

Don. On the other hand, my dear comrades, we are not to be left alone, or without help. It is more than probable that new settlers will come to our succor ere long. It is true, we are much embarrassed now by the savages, but we have also diminished their numbers. So far they have gained very little over us. We will now watch them very closely, and attend to all circumstances that give us an advantage over them. Let no man leave the fort without a rifle, and then only accompanied by another man or two. As soon as one is attacked, let all of us go to his rescue.

Jon. (*Aside.*) So if I am drunk I want you to come to my rescue.

Rob. Think of our sufferings and hardships when we were first coming here. Think of our battles won over them ! What ! give up this beautiful country, these rich lands, these growing crops, our strong fortifications, this great lick of salt that attracts numerous deer and buffaloes, these exuberant springs of fresh water, in one word, our whole new home with our mothers, wives and innocent children, and flee from all this like a pack of cowards? (*All arise.*)

DON. No, we will not flee, but stick to our property, defend our wives and children, and stand to them like *one* man, come what may—rather death than cowardly flight!

[Hurrah for our fathers, Robertson and Donaldson.]

JON. (*Aside.*) Ah! Is this the way the farce turns out? I thought you were all going to jump into the Cumberland and drown yourselves. You have fooled *me* this time, whereas fooling *you* is always my business. Just wait, it wont be long—between this and a drink, etc.

3.

TREATY OF PEACE.

(*Chief Moytoy with Indians and all the settlers sitting around under trees, one after the other smokes the Calumet, talking. Robertson gets up and makes a speech; all listen attentively.*)

ROB. My worthy Indian friends! I feel happy to see you gathered around us to-day, to listen to the Council of Peace. Alas! war has been waging long enough to the destruction of many a brave and gallant warrior on both sides. Why should there be any more blood shed between us as we are all children of the same great father, who made us all to be brothers? Let us make an end to these battles, that have made so many widows and orphans. I stand here to-day in the name of our great father, President Washington (*applause*) whose power reaches over millions of subjects, who is a real parent to his children, and who has a particular regard for his friends, the Cherokees. I have many valuable presents to make to you. He expects you, in return, to surrender a share of your territories. He demands lands to built two forts upon them in your country, to protect you against your enemies, and to be a retreat to your friends and allies. I can show you the great poverty and the wicked designs of the French, and we hope you will permit none of them to enter your villages.

(*Moytoy rises, holding his bow in one hand, his shaft of arrows and other symbols in the other.*)

Moy. What I now speak, our Father, the Great President Washington should hear. We are brothers to the people of French Lick, one great house covers us all. (*Taking a boy by the hand, he presents him to Col. Robertson, saying:*) We, our wives and our children are all children to the great President. I have brought this child, that when he grows up, he may remember our agreement this day, and to tell it to the next generation, that it may be known forever ! (*Then opening his bag of earth and laying it at the Col's. feet, says:*) We freely surrender a part of our lands to the great President. The French want our possessions, but we will defend them while one of our nation shall remain alive. (*Then showing his bow and arrows adds:*) These are all the arms we can make for our defense. We hope the President will pity his children, the Cherokees, and send us guns and ammunition. We fear not the French. Give us arms and we will go war against the enemies of the great President.

(*Taking a crown made of five eagle feathers:*)
Take this crown, which was brought here from Tennessee, our headquarters, inherited from the great chiefs, my fathers and grandfathers and lay it to the President's feet.

(*Then delivering the Col. a string of wampum, in confirmation of what he had said, he added:*)
My speech is at an end; it is the voice of the Cherokee nation. I hope the Col. will send it to the President, that it may be kept forever.

Rob. I wish that you would depute some of your chiefs to accompany you to go to Washington and do homage in person to the great President.

Jon. (*Aside.*) Gee hue! That was a great treaty, a long treaty; now I want you to treat me too and not let it take long—a long time—till you treat me again, etc.

4.

THE WEDDING.

(*All seated; Rob. stands up.*)

ROB. Dear friends and comrades: I am glad to say that peace is restored. So far, our settlement on the bluff has been going by different names. Some call it French Lick, because of the salt spring yonder in the bottom, and because it was first settled by the French. Now we must give it another definite name by which it shall be known forever, when it shall be the center of a great empire. (*Sitting down. Don. gets up.*)

DON. I propose to name it after Col. Francis Nash, who, in the battle of Germantown, commanded as Brigadier General of the regiment in the Continental army, and at the head of his brigade, fell bravely fighting for the independence of his country. (*Mansco rises.*)

MAN. I make a motion then that we call it Nashborough or Nashburg.

ROB. I think my friends will all agree with me if I propose to call her Nashville!

ALL. Hurrah for Nashville! (*Don. rises.*)

DON. I now make a motion that we name this,

our county, after that glorious comrade of Gen. Nash —Col. Davidson! (*Mansco rises.*)

MAN. I second the motion.

ROB. I am proud to state that it has been moved and seconded that we name this the county of Davidson. All as agree with this will please say so!

ALL. I—I—and I.

ROB. Contrary—no. Carried!

This great country has also had different names. It has been called "The Watauga Association," "The State of Franklin or Frankland," "Part of North Carolina," and lastly "The Territory of the United States south of the Ohio." But now, as it is destined to be a star in the great Union, she ought to have a permanent and innate name.

DON. I make the proposition that we name her after that chief's village in the east of this State, the headquarters of the Cherokee nation, where that celebrated crown of five eagle's feathers was brought from, which this venerable old chief to-day laid to the feet of our great President Washington, and after which our principal river is already named—Tenassee.

ALL. Seconded—carried—Hail to Tenassee!

ROB. And now my most dear friends, I have to perform my last and most pleasant duty yet. Having made a treaty with the Indians and pacified them so that we can live unmolested in future, and, whereas, my very best and bravest associate here, Col. John Donaldson has applied for the hand of my beloved daughter, whom he has rescued so gallantly from the hands of the savages with peril of his own life, and,. whereas, the Governor of this great State [Jon. (*aside*) I now begin to see the Governors in their true light. I'm sure they are the best fellows in the world!] has invested me with the power of solemnizing the rites of matrimony, therefore I, Jas. Robertson join thee, Col. John Donaldson and thee, Elizabeth Robertson in the bands of holy matrimony, and declare you to be lawful husband and wife!

ALL. Good luck! Hurrah! (*Exeunt.*)

JON. (*Aside.*) Bully for you! I always thought the whole farce would end with a wedding. Now we have it! But now let them rip; as for myself, I'll go on a big spree. Long live the Governors of North and South Carolina! Hussa!

Exit.

PART 2.

A HISTORICAL SKETCH

OF

Cols. Robertson and Donaldson

AND THEIR ASSOCIATES IN

THE FOUNDATION OF NASHVILLE

IN 1780,

ACCORDING TO

Ramsey's Annals of Tennessee.

DISCOVERY OF TENNESSEE.

When the first white explorers came to this part of the country, it was occupied by the Shawnee, Chickasaw, Uchee, Muskogee (or Creek) and Cherokee Indians, whose hunting grounds it was, but who had no regular settlements here. But before them there were other nations here, who had been driven away or extipated by these Indians. The latter acknowledged this, and named them at a very noted congress or treaty, held early in the last century at Lancaster, Pa., the "Conyuch—such—roona" and similar barbarous names. A proof of this are their relics, which we still possess, consisting of forts, cemeteries, tumuli, temples and altars, camps, towns, videttes and fortifications. Around the present site of Nashville, there was at every lasting spring a large collection of graves, made in a peculiar way, the whole covered with a stratum of mould or dirt, eight or ten inches deep. At many springs is the appearance of walls, enclosing ancient habitations, the foundations of which were visible whenever the earth was cleared and cultivated—to these walls entrenchments were sometimes added. The walls sometimes enclose six, eight or ten acres of land, and sometimes they are more extensive.

These structures were not erected by the more

modern Indians, but furnish unquestionable evidence that a dense population, at a remote period, occupied this country and had some progress in the arts of civilized life.

The Indians had driven other nations away, but were unwilling to give up those grounds to the whites in their turn. Often they shouted: "Keep on, robbers and traitors; in Acuera and Apalachee we will treat you as you deserve. Every captive we will quarter and hang upon the highest trees along the road." (Irving.)

It is uncertain who were the first whites that crossed the wilderness. Martin suggests that Ferd. De Soto, a Spanish adventurer, authorized by Charles V. in 1539, entered the Southern part of East Tennessee, came across and left it near Memphis over the Mississippi. In 1673, Marquette came down this river and built the first cabin and fort on Chickasaw Bluff. Later on La Salle erected a trading post near the same place in 1682.

Before 1714, the Shawnees had conquered the Chickasaws and driven them away from where Nashville now stands. The same year M. Charleville, a French trader from Crozat's colony at New Orleans came here. His store was built upon a mound, on the west side of Cumberland river, near French Lick Creek, and about seventy yards from each stream. M. Charleville thus planted upon the banks of the

Cumberland the germs of civilization and commerce, unconscious that it contained the seminal principle of future wealth, consequence and empire.

The French first claimed Tennessee, and in fact the whole Mississippi valley and its tributaries.

The English, through Sir A. Cummings, treated with the Cherokees, their chief Moytoy representing these, for lands, trading and their general assistance. At such an instance, in 1730, the name Tennessee was first mentioned as the headquarter village where the crown of that chief was brought from. The village was situated on the west bank of a river of the same name (the Little Tennessee.) The main stream, of which this is a tributary, received its name from that town.

In 1739. Fort Assumption was built on Memphis Bluff. The first fort built by the Anglo-Americans was Fort Loudon on Tennessee river in 1756.

Dr. Walker, passing Powell's valley, gave the name of "Cumberland" to the lofty range of mountains on the West. Tracing this range in a southwestern direction, he came to a remarkable depression in the chain which he called "Cumberland Gap." On the Western side of the range he found a beautiful mountain stream which he named "Cumberland River," all in honor of the Duke of Cumberland, then Prime Minister of England. These names were ever since retained, and, with Loudon, are believed to be the only names in Tennessee of English origin. (Ramsey.)

The first Irish immigrants came here through Delaware Bay, others by the port of Charleston.

The Aborigines named the Tennessee River "Kalamuchee" from its confluence with the Ohio to the mouth of Little Tennessee. From this point to the mouth of French Broad, it was called "Cootla," and from there to the mouth of Watauga, the Holston was known to the Indians as "Hogohegee." Little River was the "Canot," Cumberland was called by Indians "Warioto."

Previous to the Watauga settlers, Daniel Boon, a hunter from Yadkin, N. C., entered Tennessee, according to an inscription, still to be seen on a beech tree near the road from Jonesborough to Blountville.

D. Boon
CillED A. BAR On
Tree
in THE
yEAR
1760.

The first grant of lands was made in 1756, by the authorities of Virginia to E. Pendleton, comprising 3,000 acres of ground lying in Augusta county, on a branch of the middle fork of the Indian River, called West Creek, now Sullivan County, Tennessee.

WATAUGA.

Watauga River derived its name from Watauga town, an ancient Indian village, occupying the present Elizabethtown, Carter County. It is a tributary to the Tennessee River.

The white settlement here originated by immigrants coming from Wake County, N. C.,—G. Christian, W. Anderson and Col. J. Sawyers were among the first. Capt. W. Bean came from Pennsylvania County, Virginia, and settled on Boon's Creek, (1769.) Carter County received its name from Capt. Carter. Boon (D.) came to Watauga in 1769. In 1770, Jas. Robertson came from Wake County and lived here.

The first white female that came to Watauga was Mrs. Boon, in 1773.

Russel Bean was the first white child born in Tennessee.

The first mill erected was at Buffalo Creek, built by B. M'Nabb.

As early as 1772, a congregation was organized and a church built among these primitive people, to whom the Rev. Chas. Cummings preached.

The Legislature of North Carolina, in 1779, laid off and established Jonesborough as the seat of justice for what was then Washington County.

T. Sharp, Spencer and others, allured by the flattering accounts they had received of the fertility of the soil and of the abundance of game which the country afforded, determined to visit it. They came 1776 to Cumberland River and built a number of cabins. Most of them returned, leaving Spencer and Holliday, who remained in the country till 1779.

Capt. De Mumbreune who, as late as 1823, lived in Nashville, hunted in that country as early as 1775.

In 1778, the first plantation was fixed on the Cumberland. A small field of corn was planted in the spring 1778, near Bledsoe's Creek. A large hollow tree stood near the lick. In this Spencer lived. He was pleased with the prospects for further settlement which the situation afforded, and could not be induced to relinquish them and return home, as Holliday in vain persuaded him to do. The latter, however, determined to leave the wilderness, but having lost his knife, was unwilling to undertake his long travel without one with which to skin his venison and cut his meat. With backwoods generosity and kindness, Spencer accompanied his comrade to the barrens of Kentucky, put him on the right path, broke his knife and gave him half of it, and returned to his hollow tree at the lick, where he passed the winter. Spencer was a man of gigantic stature, and passing one morning the temporary cabin erected at a place since called Eaton's Station, and occupied by one of Capt. De Mumbreune's hunters, his huge tracks were left plainly impressed in the rich alluvial. These were seen by the hunter on his return to the camp, who, alarmed at their size, immediately swam across the river, and wandered through the woods until he reached the French settlements on the Wabash.

(*See Ramsey's Annals of Tennessee.*)

CAPT. ROBERTSON'S FIRST COLONY AT FRENCH LICK.

Nearly ten years had now elapsed since the germ of a civilized community had been planted in upper East Tennessee. No settlement had been permanently fixed on the lower Cumberland. A hunter's camp and the lonely habitation of Spencer were all that relieved the solitude or lighted the gloom of that western wilderness. But the cheerlessness of barbarian night was about to be dissipated by the dawn of civilization and improvement. In the early spring of 1779, a little colony of gallant adventurers, from the parent hive at Watauga, crossed the Cumberland Mountains, penetrated the intervening wilds, and pitched their tents near the French Lick and planted a field of corn where the city of Nashville now stands. This field was near the lower ferry. These pioneers were Capt. James Robertson, George Freeland, William Neely, Edward Swanson, Jas. Hanly, Mark Robertson, Zach. White and Will Overhall. A negro also accompanied them. To their number was added, immediately after their arrival at the Lick, a number of others conducted by Mansco, who had ten years before visited and explored, and hunted in the country. These emigrants also planted corn preparatory to the removal of their families in the succeeding autumn. Capt. Robertson, during the summer, went to Illinois to purchase the cabin rights from Gen. Clarke. After the crop was made, Overhall, White and Swanson, were left to keep the buffaloes out of the unenclosed fields of corn, while the rest of the party returned for their families.

Mansco, Frazier and other early hunters and explorers, upon their previous return to the older settlements, had diffused an account of the fertility of the Cumberland lands, the abundance of game and the salubrity of the climate. This account was now confirmed and extended by the experiments that had been made by the parties under Robertson and Mansco in planting and raising a crop. Cumberland became the theme of eager conversation in every neighborhood, and great numbers prepared to emigrate to this land of future plenty and promise. Under the lead of Mansco, several families removed and settled at Mansco's Lick, Bledsoe's Lick and other places. John Rains and others, in October of this year (1779,) leaving New River, on their way to Kentucky, were persuaded by Robertson to accompany him to the French Lick. Assenting to this proposal, they were soon joined by several other companies of emigrants —the whole amounting to two or three hundred—

some of them took out cattle and other domestic animals. The route pursued was by Cumberland Gap, and the Kentucky trace to Whitley's Station, on the waters of Green River; thence to Robertson's Fork, on the north side of that stream; thence down the river to Pitman's Station; thence crossing and descending that river to Little Barren, crossing it at the Elk Lick; thence passing the Blue Spring and the Dripping Spring to Big Barren; thence up Drake's Creek to a bituminous spring; thence to the Maple Swamp; thence the Red River at Kilgore's Station; thence to Mansco's Creek, and from there to the French Lick.—[From Ramsey.]

The inclemency of the season, the great number of the emigrants, the delay inseparable from travelling over a new route, part of it mountainous, all of it through a wilderness, without roads, bridges or ferries, prevented the arrival of the Cumberland colonists at their point of destination till the beginning of the year 1780. The winter had been intensely cold, and has always been remembered and referred to as the "cold winter" by all the countries in the northern hemisphere, and is decisive of the chronology that fixes the arrival of these emigrants in Seventeen Hundred and Eighty. The Cumberland was found frozen over. Snow had fallen early in November, and it continued to freeze for many weeks after the emigrants reached the bluff. Some of them settled on the north side of the river, at Eaton's Station, where Page afterwards resided. The following were among them: Fred Stump, A. Eaton, H. Wells, T. Roundsever, W. Loggins and Mr. Winters. Here they built cabins, cleared ground and planted corn. The cabins were built with stockades from one to the other, with port holes and bastions. But most of the company crossed immediately after their arrival over the river upon the ice and settled at the Bluff where Nashville now stands. They were admonished by the existing condition of things in the other places, the hostilities they had witnessed from the Cherokees, that their settlement could not long escape the aggression of the savages around them. They prudently erected block-houses in lines—the intervals between which were stockaded—two lines were built parallel to each other, and so were the other two lines, the whole forming a square within. Freeland's Station, where McGavock since resided, was at this time also erected. Here were also block-houses and stockades. Mr. Rains settled the place since known as Deaderick plantation. Among the emigrants that built their cabins at the Bluff, were some from South Carolina. These were J. Buchanan, Al. Buchanan, D. Williams, J. Mulherrin, Jas. Mulherrin, S. Williams, Th. Thompson, besides others.

While Robertson and his co-emigrants were thus reaching Cumberland by the circuitous and dangerous trace through the wilderness of Kentucky, others of their countrymen were undergoing greater hardships, enduring greater sufferings, and experiencing greater privations upon another route, not less circuitous and far more perilous in aiming at the same destination. Soon after the former had left the Holston settlements, on their march by land, several boats loaded with emigrants and their property left Fort Patrick Henry, near Long Island, on a voyage down the Holston and Tennessee, and up the Ohio and Cumberland. The Journal of one of them, "The Adventure," has been preserved. It was kept by Col. John Donaldson, the projector of the enterprise. The original is still in possession of the descendants of his family. The details of so new and remarkable an adventure by water are full of interest, and the journal is, therefore, given entire:

"JOURNAL OF A VOYAGE, intended by God's permission, in the good boat Adventure, from Fort Patrick Henry on Holston River, to the French Salt Springs on Cumberland River, kept by John Donaldson.

December 22, 1779.—Took our departure from the fort and fell down the river to the mouth of Reedy Creek, where we were stopped by the fall of water, and most excessive hard frost; and after much delay and difficulties we arrived at the mouth of Cloud's Creek, on Sunday evening, the 20th February, 1780, where we lay by until Sunday, 28th, when we took our departure with sundry other vessels bound for the same voyage, and on the same day struck the Poor Valley Shoal, together with Mr. Boyd and Mr. Rounsifer, on which shoal we lay that afternoon and succeeding night in much distress.

Monday, February 28th, 1780.—In the morning the water rising, we got off the shoal, after landing thirty persons to lighten our boat. In attempting to land on an island, received some damage and lost sundry articles, and came to camp on the south shore, where we joined sundry other vessels also bound down.

Tuesday 29th.—Proceeded down the river and camped on the north shore, the afternoon and following day proving rainy.

Wednesday, March 1st.—Proceeded on and camped on the south shore, nothing happening that day remarkable.

March 2d.—Rain about half the day; passed the mouth of French Broad River, and about 12 o'clock Mr. Henry's boat being driven on the point of an island† by the force of the current was sunk, the whole cargo much damaged and the crew's lives much endangered, which occasioned the whole fleet to put on shore and go to their assistance, but with much difficulty bailed her, in order to take in her cargo again. The same afternoon Reuben Harrison

---
†Probably William's Island, two miles above Knoxville.

went out a hunting and did not return that night, though many guns were fired to fetch him in.

Friday, 3.—Early in the morning fired a four-pounder for the lost man, sent out sundry persons to search the woods for him, firing many guns that day and the succeeding night, but all without success, to the great grief of his parents and fellow travellers.

Saturday, 4th.—Proceeded on our voyage, leaving old Mr. Harrison with some other vessels to make further search for his lost son; about ten o'clock the same day found him a considerable distance down the river, where Mr. Ben. Belew took him on board his boat. At 2 o'clock, P. M., passed the mouth of Tennessee River, and camped on the south shore about ten miles below the mouth of Tennessee.

Sunday, 5th.—Cast off and got under way before sunrise; 12 o'clock passed the mouth of Clinch; at 12 o'clock M., came up with the Clinch River Company, whom we joined and camped, the evening proving rainy.

Monday, 6th.—Got under way before sunrise; the morning proving very foggy, many of the fleet were much bogged—about 10 o'clock lay by for them: when collected, proceeded down. Camped on the north shore, where Capt. Hutching's negro man died, being much frosted in his feet and legs, of which he died.

Tuesday, 7th.—Got under way very early, the day

proving very windy, a S.S.W., and the river being wide occasioned a high sea, insomuch that some of the smaller crafts were in danger; therefore came to, at the uppermost Chiccamauga Town, which was then evacuated, where we lay by that afternoon and camped that night. The wife of Ephraim Peyton was here delivered of a child. Mr. Peyton has gone through by land with Capt. Robertson.

Wednesday, 8th.—Cast off at 10 o'clock, and proceed down to an Indian village, which was inhabited, on the south side of the river; they insisted on us to "come ashore," called us brothers, and showed other signs of friendship, insomuch that Mr. John Caffery and my son then on board took a canoe which I had in tow, and were crossing over to them, the rest of the fleet having landed on the opposite shore. After they had gone some distance, a half-breed, who called himself Archy Coody, with several other Indians, jumped into a canoe, met them, and advised them to return to the boat, which they did, together with Coody and several canoes which left the shore and followed directly after him. They appeared to be friendly. After distributing some presents among them, with which the seemed much pleased, we observed a number of Indians on the other side embarking in their canoes, armed and painted with red and black. Coody immediately made signs to his companions, ordering them to quit the boat, which they did, himself and another Indian remaining with us and telling us to move off instantly. We had not gone far before we discovered a number of Indians armed and painted proceeding down the river, as it were, to intercept us. Coody, the half-breed, and his companion, sailed with us for some time, and telling us that we had passed all the towns and were out of danger, left us. But we had not gone far until we had come in sight of another town, situated likewise on the south side of the river, nearly opposite a small island. Here they again invited us to come on shore, called us brothers, and observing the boats standing off for the opposite channel, told us that "their side of the river was better for boats to pass." And here we must regret the unfortunate death of young Mr. Payne, on board Capt. Blackemore's boat, who was mortally wounded by reason of the boat running too near the northern shore opposite the town, where some of the enemy lay concealed, and the more tragical misfortune of poor Stuart, his family and friends to the number of twenty-eight persons. This man had embarked with us for the Western country, but his family being diseased with the smallpox, it was agreed upon between him and the company that he should keep at some distance in the rear, for fear of the infection spreading, and he was warned each night when the encampment should take place by the sound of a horn. After we had passed the town, the Indians having now collected to a considerable number, observing his helpless situation, singled off from the rest of the fleet, intercepted him and killed and took prisoners the whole crew, to the great grief of the whole company, uncertain how soon they might share the same fate; their cries were distinctly heard by those boats in the rear.

We still perceived them marching down the river in considerable bodies, keeping pace with us until the Cumberland Mountain withdrew them from our sight, when we were in hopes we had escaped them. We were now arrived at the place called the Whirl or Suck, where the river is compressed within less than its common width above, by the Cumberland Mountain, which juts in on both sides. In passing through the upper part of these narrows, at a place described by Coody, which he termed the "boiling pot," a trivial accident had nearly ruined the expedition. One of the company, John Cotton, who was moving down in a large canoe, had attached it to Robert Cartwright's boat, into which he and his family had gone for safety. The canoe was here overturned, and the little cargo lost. The company pitying his distress, concluded to halt and assist him in recovering his property. They had landed on the northern shore at a level spot, and were going up to the place, when the Indians, to our astonishment, appeared immediately over us on the opposite cliffs, and commenced firing down upon us, which occasioned a precipitate retreat to the boats. We immediately moved off, the Indians lining the bluffs along continued their fire from the heights on our boats below, without doing any other injury than wounding four slightly. Jenning's boat is missing.

We have now passed through the Whirl. The river widens with a placid and gentle current; and all the company appear to be in safety except the family of Jonathan Jennings, whose boat ran on a large rock, projecting out from the northern shore, and partly immersed in water immediately at the Whirl, where we were compelled to leave them, perhaps to be slaughtered by their merciless enemies. Continued to sail on that day and floated throughout the following night.

Thursday, 9th.—Proceeded on our journey, nothing happening worthy attention to-day; floated till about midnight, and encamped on the northern shore.

Friday, 10th.—This morning about 4 o'clock we were surprised by the cries of "help poor Jennings," at some distance in the rear. He had discovered us by our fires, and come up in the most wretched condition. He states, that as soon as the Indians discovered his situation they turned their whole attention to him, and kept up a most galling fire at his boat. He ordered his wife, a son nearly grown, a young man who accompanied them and his negro man and woman, to throw all his goods into the river, to lighten their boat for the purpose of getting her off, himself returning their fire as well as he could, being a good soldier and an excellent marksman. But before they had accomplished their object, his son, the young man and the negro, jumped out of the boat and left them. He thinks the young man and the negro were wounded before they left the boat.* Mrs. Jennings, however, and the negro woman, succeeded in unloading the boat, but chiefly by the exertions of Mrs. Jennings, who got out of the boat and shoved her off, but was near falling a victim to her own intrepidity on account of the boat starting so suddenly as soon as loosened from the rock. Upon examination, he appears to have made a wonderful escape, for his boat is pierced in numberless places with bullets. It is to be remarked, that Mrs. Peyton, who was the night before delivered of an infant, which was unfortunately killed upon the hurry and confusion consequent upon such a disaster, assisted them, being frequently exposed to wet and cold then and afterwards, and that her health appears to be good at this time,

---

*The negro was drowned. The son and the young man swam to the north side of the river, where they found and embarked in a canoe and floated down the river. The next day they were met by canoes full of Indians, who took them prisoners and carried them to Chickamauga, where they killed and burned the young men. They knocked Jennings down and were about to kill him, but were prevented by the friendly mediation of Rogers, an Indian trader, who ransomed him with goods. Rogers had been taken prisoner by Sevier a short time before, and had been released; and that good office he requited by the ransom of Jennings.

and I think and hope she will do well. Their clothes were very much cut with bullets, especially Mrs. Jennings's.

Saturday, 11*th*.—Got under way after having distributed the family of Mrs. Jennings in the other boats. Rowed on quietly that day, and encamped for the night on the north shore.

Sunday, 12*th*.—Set out, and after a few hours sailing we heard the crowing of cocks, and soon came within view of the town; here they fired on us again without doing any injury.

After running until about 10 o'clock, came in sight of the Muscles Shoals. Halted on the northern shore at the appearance of the shoals, in order to search for the signs Capt. James Robertson was to make for us at that place. He set out from Holston early in the fall of 1779, was to proceed by the way of Kentucky to the Big Salt Lick on Cumberland River, with several others in company, was to come across from the Big Salt Lick to the upper end of the shoals, there to make such signs that we might know he had been there, and that it was practicable for us to go across by land. But to our great mortification we can find none—from which we conclude that it would not be prudent to make the attempt, and are determined, knowing ourselves to be in such imminent danger, to pursue our journey down the river. After trimming our boats in the best manner possible, we ran through the shoals before night. When we approached them they had a dreadful appearance to those who had never seen them before. The water being high made a terrible roaring, which could be heard at some distance among the drift-wood heaped frightfully upon the points of the islands, the current running in every possible direction. Here we did not know how soon we should be dashed to pieces and all our troubles ended at once. Our boats frequently dragged on the bottom, and appeared constantly in danger of striking. They warped as much as in a rough sea. But by the hand of Providence we are now preserved from this danger also. I know not the length of this wonderful shoal; it had been represented to me to be 25 or 30 miles. If so, we must have descended very rapidly, as indeed we did, for we passed it in about three hours. Came to, and camped on the northern shore, not far below the shoals, for the night.

Monday, 13*th.*—Got under way early in the morning, and made a good run that day.

Tuesday, 14*th.*—Set out early. On this day two boats approaching too near the shore, were fired on by the Indians. Five of the crews were wounded, but none dangerously. Came to camp at night near the mouth of a creek. After kindling fires, and preparing for rest, the company were alarmed, on account of the incessant barking our dogs kept up taking it for granted that the Indians were attempting to surprise, we retreated precipitately to the boats; fell down the river about a mile and encamped on the other shore. In the morning I prevailed on Mr. Caffrey and my son to cross below in a canoe, and return to the place; which they did, and found an African negro we had left in the hurry, asleep by one of the fires. The voyagers returned and collected their utensils which had been left.

Wednesday, 15*th.*—Got under way and moved on peaceably the five following days, when we arrived at the mouth of the Tennessee on Monday, the 20th, and landed on the lower point immediately on the bank of the Ohio. Our situation here is truly disagreeable. The river is very high, and the current rapid, our boats not constructed for the purpose of stemming a rapid stream, our provision exhausted, the crews almost worn down with hunger and fatigue, and know not what distance we have to go, or what time it will take us to our place of destination. The scene is rendered still more melancholy, as several boats will not attempt to ascend the rapid current. Some intend to descend the Mississippi to Natchez; others are bound for the Illinois—among the rest my son-in-law and daughter. We now part, perhaps to meet no more, for I am determined to pursue my course, happen what will.

Tuesday, 21*st.*—Set out, and on this day labored

very hard and got but a little way; camped on the south bank of the Ohio. Passed the two following days as the former, suffering much from hunger and fatigue.

Friday, 24th.—About 3 o'clock came to the mouth of a river which I thought was the Cumberland. Some of the company declared it could not be—it was so much smaller than we expected. But I never heard of any river running in between the Cumberland and Tennessee. It appeared to flow with a gentle current. We determined, however, to make the trial, pushed up some distance and encamped for the night.

Saturday, 25.—To-day we are much encouraged; the river grows wider; the current is very gentle, and we are now convinced it is the Cumberland. I have derived great assistance from a small square sail which was fixed up on the day we left the mouth of the river; and to prevent any ill-effects from sudden flaws of wind, a man was stationed at each of the lower corners of the sheet, with directions to give way whenever it was necessary.

Sunday, 26th.—Got under way early; procured some buffalo meat; though poor it was palatable.

Monday, 27th.—Set out again; killed a swan, which was very delicious.

Tuesday, 28th.—Set out very early this morning; killed some buffalo.

Wednesday, 29th.—Proceeded up the river; gathered some herbs on the bottoms of Cumberland, which some of the company called Shawnee salad.

Thursday, 30th.—Proceeded on our voyage. This day we killed some more buffalo.

Friday, 31st.—Set out this day, and after running some distance, met with Col. Richard Henderson, who was running the line between Virginia and North Carolina. At this meeting we were much rejoiced. He gave us every information we wished, and further informed us that he had purchased a quantity of corn in Kentucky, to be shipped at the Falls of Ohio for the use of the Cumberland Settlement. We are now without bread, and are compelled to hunt the buffalo to preserve life. Worn out with fatigue, our progress at present is slow. Camped at night near the mouth of a little river, at which place and below there is a handsome bottom of rich land. Here we found a pair of hand-mill stones set up for grinding, but appeared not to have been used for a great length of time.

Proceeded on quietly until the 12th of April, at which time we came to the mouth of a little river running in on the north side, by Moses Renfoe and his company called Red River, up which they intend to settle. Here they took leave of us. We proceeded up Cumberland, nothing happening material until the 23d, when we reached the first settlement on the north side of the river, one mile and a half below the Big Salt Lick and called Eaton's Station, after a man of that name, who, with several other families, came through Kentucky and settled there.

Monday, April 24th.—This day we arrived at our journey's end at the Big Salt Lick, where we have the pleasure of finding Capt. Robertson and his company. It is a source of satisfaction to us to be enabled to restore to him and others their families and friends, who were entrusted to our care, and who, sometime since, perhaps, despaired of ever meeting again. Though our prospects at present are dreary, we have found a few log cabins which have been built on a cedar bluff above the Lick, by Capt. Robertson and his company."

(1780.) The distance traversed in the island voyage, the extreme danger from the navigation of the rapid and unknown rivers, and the hostile attacks from the savages upon their banks, mark the emigration under Col. Donaldson as one of the greatest achievements in the settlement of the West. The names of these adventurous navigators and bold pioneers of the Cumberland country are not, all of them, recollected; some of them follow: Mrs. Robertson, the wife of James Robertson, Col. Donaldson, John Donaldson, Jun., Robert Cartwright, Benjamin Porter, James Cain, Isaac Neely, John Cotton, Mr. Rounsever, Jonathan Jennings, William Crutchfield,

Moses Renfroe, Joseph Renfroe, James Renfroe, Solomon Turpin, —— Johns, Sen., Francis Armstrong, Isaac Lanier, Daniel Dunham, John Boyd, John Montgomery, John Cockrill and John Caffrey, with their respective families; also, Mary Henry, a widow, and her family, Mary Purnell and her family, John Blackmore and John Gibson.

These, with the emigrants already mentioned as having arrived with Robertson by the way of Kentucky trace, and the few that had remained at the Bluff to take care of the growing crops, constituted the nucleus of the Cumberland community in 1780. Some of them plunged, at once, into the adjoining forests, and built a cabin with its necessary defences. Col. Donaldson, himself, with his connections, was of this number. He went up the Cumberland and settled upon Stone's River, a confluent of that stream, at a place since called Clover Bottom, where he erected a small fort on its south side. The situation was found to be too low, as the water, during a freshet, surrounded the fort, and it was, for that reason, removed to the north side.

Dr. Walker, the Commissioner on the part of Virginia, for running the boundary line between that State and North Carolina, arrived at the Bluff. He was accompanied by Col. Richard Henderson and his two brothers, Nathaniel and Pleasant. Col. Henderson erected a station also, on Stone's river, and re mained there some time, selling lands under the deed made to himself and partners by the Cherokees, at Watauga, in March, 1775, as has been already mentioned. He sold one thousand acres per head at ten dollars per thousand. His certificate entitled the holder, at a future time, to further proceedings in a land office.* The purchase of "Transylvania in America," as made by Henderson and his associates, without any authority from the States of North Carolina and Virginia, was, in itself, null and void, so far as it claimed to vest the title of lands in those individuals. The associates could be recognized only as private citizens, having no right to make treaties with or purchase lands from the Indians. This treaty was, however, considered as an extinguishment of the Indian title to the lands embraced within the boundaries mentioned in it. The legislatures of the two States, for this reason, and as a remuneration for the expenditures previous and subsequent to the treaty of Watauga, allowed, to the Transylvania Company, a grant of two hundred thousand acres from each State.

One of the great sources of Indian invasion and of hostile instigation, had been broken up by the capture of the British posts on the Wabash and in the Illinois country, and the captivity of Col. Hamilton, who was now a prisoner at Williamsburg. Many of the western tribes, had entered into treaties of peace and

---
*Haywood.

friendship with Col. Clarke, which presaged a temporary quietude to the frontier people. The repeated chastisements of the Cherokees by the troops under Sevier and Shelby, seemed, for a time, to secure the friendship of that nation. The news of this condition of western affairs gave a new impulse to emigration, and the roads and traces to Kentucky and Cumberland were crowded with hardy adventurers, seeking home and fortune in their distant wilds. This rapid increase of population exhausted the limited supply of food in the country, and a dearth ensued. Corn, and every other article of family consumption, became remarkably scarce. The winter had been long and exceedingly cold. The cattle and hogs designed for the use of the emigrants in their new settlements, had perished from starvation and the inclemency of the season. The game in the woods was, from like causes, poor and sickly, and, though easily found and taken, was unfit for food. This scarcity prevailed throughout the whole frontier line for five hundred miles, and was aggravated by the circumstance that no source of supply was within the reach of the suffering people. In the neighboring settlements of Kentucky, corn was worth, in March of 1780, one hundred and sixty-five dollars a bushel, in continental money, which price it maintained until the opening spring supplied other means of sustenance.*

---
*Monette.

Such were the circumstances under which the pioneers of the Lower Cumberland formed the first permanent white settlement in Middle Tennessee. Their position was that of hardship and danger, toil and suffering. As has been well said by another† in reference to Kentucky: they were posted in the heart of the most favorite hunting ground of numerous and hostile tribes of Indians on the north and on the south ; a ground endeared to them by its profusion of the finest game, subsisting on the luxuriant vegetation of this great natural park, It was, emphatically, the Eden of the Red Man. Was it then wonderful, that all his fiercest passions and wildest energies, should be aroused in its defence, against an enemy, whose success was the Indian's downfall?

The little band of emigrants at the Bluff were in the center of a vast wilderness, equi-distant from the most war-like and ferocious tribes on this continent— tribes that had frequently wasted the frontiers of Carolina, Virginia and Pennsylvania, with the tomahawk and with fire, and that were now aided, in the unnatural alliance of Great Britain, by the arts and treasures furnished by the agents of that government. To attack and invasion from these tribes, the geographical position of the Cumberland settler gave a peculiar exposure and a special liability. Three hundred miles of wilderness separated them from the nearest fort of their countrymen on Holston. They were,

---
†Butler.

perhaps, double that distance from their seat of government in North Carolina, while all the energies of the parent States were employed in the tremendous struggle for Independence, in the cause of which she had so early and so heartily engaged. This forlorn situation of the settlement at the Bluff became more perilous, as it was so accessible by water from the distant hostile tribes. Descending navigation could bring, with great rapidity, the fleets of canoes and perogues, from the Ohio and its western tributaries, loaded with the armed warriors of that region; while upon the Tennessee River, with equal celerity, the Cherokee and Creek braves could precipitate themselves to the different landings on that stream, and co-operating with their confederates from the north, unite in one general stroke of devastation and havoc. Had this been done at the period of the first emigration, the Bluff settlement could have been annihilated. Happily, the protracted and inclement winter that inflicted its inhospitable severity and such great hardships upon the first emigrants, protected them from attack, by confining their enemies to their towns and wigwams. Early in January, a small party of Delaware Indians came from the direction of the Cany Fork, and passed by the head of Mill Creek, and encamped on one of its branches, which has since been called Indian Creek. The Indians proceeded to Bear Creek of Tennessee, and continued there during the summer. At this time they offered no molestation to the whites. Before the next irruption of the Indians, time was given for the erection of defences, and Robertson's second colony was planted—consisting, like the first at Watauga, of intrepid men and and heroic women—fit elements for the foundation of a great and flourishing State. And here, at the Bluff, with its little garrison and rude stations—in the centre of a wide wilderness, and overshadowed by huge evergreens and the ancient forest around it—amidst the snows, and ice, and storms of 1780, was fixed the seat of commerce, of learning and the arts —the future abode of refinement and hospitality, and the cradle of empire.

When the first settlers came to the Bluff in 1779--'80, Haywood says the country had the appearance of one which had never before been cultivated. There was no sign of any cleared land, nor other appearance of former cultivation. Nothing was presented to the eye but one large plain of woods and cane, frequented by buffaloes, elk, deer, wolves, foxes, panthers and other animals suited to the climate. The lands adjacent to the French Lick, which Mansco, in 1769, when he first hunted here, called an old field, was a large open space, frequented and trodden by buffaloes, whose large paths led to it from all parts of the country and there concentred. On these adjacent lands was no under-growth nor cane, as far as the water reached in time of high water. The country as far as to Elk River and beyond it, had not a single permanent inhabitant, except the wild beasts of the forest; but there were traces, as everywhere else, of having been inhabited many centuries before by a numerous population.

CUMBERLAND—THE FRANKLIN COUNTIES.

A young brave, at the treaty of Watauga, was overheard by the interpreter, to urge, in support of the Transylvania cession, this argument: that the settlement and occupancy of the ceded territory, by the whites, would interpose an impregnable barrier between the Northern and Southern Indians, and that the latter would, in future, have quiet and undisturbed possession of the choice hunting grounds south of the Cumbertand. His argument prevailed against the prophetic warning and eloquent remonstrance of Occonostota. That aged chieftain, covered over with scars, the evidence of many a hard-fought battle for the Dark and Bloody Ground, signed the treaty reluctantly, and taking Daniel Boon by the hand, said, with most significant earnestness: "Brother, we have given you a fine land, but I believe you will have much trouble in settling it;" words of ominous import, as subsequent events too mournfully proved. These events, so far as the pioneers of Tennessee were engaged in them, will now be narrated. "Much trouble," indeed was experienced in settling the ceded country, and that adjoining it. Instead of serving as a barrier between the common claimants, the settlers became a central point of attack—a target at which the surrounding tribes all aimed their deadliest shot.

We left the colony of Robertson and others, near the French Lick, at the end of a protracted and severe winter. The opening spring enabled the savages to resume hostilities. The whole line of frontier, from Pennsylvania to Georgia, was simultaneously assailed by marauding parties of Indians, distributed along its entire extent. Terror and consternation were only the precursors of havoc and desolation. The leading chiefs of the Shawnee tribe, which had once held possession of the Cumberland Valley, were unremitting in their efforts to bring about a general concert of action among all the northwestern tribes, for a grand exterminating invasion, during the next summer. In this they had the approbation and encouragement of British agents and officers, at Detroit and on the Maumee, who assured them of the powerful aid of their great ally, George III.* Similar influences were constantly at work with the southern tribes; and in addition to these general causes of dissatisfaction and hostility, Fort Jefferson had been built, the previous year, in the territory of the Chickasaws, without their consent, and the chief, Colbert,

---

*Monette.

prepared to repel the invaders by force. The proximity of this tribe to the Cumberland settlement, was cause of serious apprehension and alarm. But the first assault upon the Cumberland settlers was made by the southern Indians—the Cherokees and Creeks. They seized the first opportunity after the *hard winter* was over, to approach the "improvements" around the Bluff, and to carry amongst the settlers the work of massacre and devastation. We abridge from Haywood and "The Museum," an account of it:

In the month of April, (1780) Keywood and Milliken, two hunters, coming to the fort, stopped on Richland Creek, five or six miles from the Bluff, and as one of them stepped down to the creek to drink, the Indians fired upon and killed Milliken. Keywood, escaping, brought intelligence of the affair to the fort. Mr. Rains then moved to the Bluff, where he continued four years before he could venture again to settle in the country. The Indians soon after killed Joseph Hay on the Lick Branch, and a party of them invested Freeland's Station, and finding an old man, Bernard, making an improvement, at what was then called Denton's Lick, killed him, cut off his head, and carried it away. With the old man were two small boys, Joseph and William Dunham, who escaped unhurt and gave the alarm to the people at Freeland's. A young man, Milliken, between the fort and Denton's Lick, not having heard the alarm, was surprised by the Indians, killed, and his head, also, was cut off and carried away. The murderers were either Creeks or Cherokees.

Soon afterwards, in July or August, a party of Indians, believed to be Delawares, killed Jonathan Jennings, at the point of the first island above Nashville. Higher up the Cumberland River, on the north side, on the bluff where William Williams, Esq., since lived, Ned Garver was killed; his wife and two children escaped, and came to Nashville. The same party, in a day or two after, killed William Neely, at Neely's Lick, and took his daughter prisoner.

At Eaton's Station, they also killed James Mayfield, near the place where, previously, Porter had been shot in the daytime by the Indians in the cedars, in view of the station. In November or December, they shot Jacob Stump, and attempted to kill the old man, Frederic Stump, but he reached the station in safety, after being pursued by the Indians three miles. At Mansco's Lick, Jesse Balestine and John Shockley were killed. In the winter of the same year, David Goin and Risby Kennedy were killed at the same place, and Mansco's Station was broken up; some of its inhabitants went to Nashville, and others to Kentucky. At Bledsoe's Lick, or on the creek near it, two persons were killed : W. Johnston and Daniel Mungle, hunting together on Barren River, the former was killed, and the latter escaped by flight.

Late in this year, a company of Indians tried to intercept Thomas Sharp Spencer, returning to the Bluff with several horses loaded with meat, after a successful hunt. They fired at, but missed him. The horses were captured, and with their cargo, were taken up the river.

At Station-Camp Creek, the same Indians took other horses, that had strayed from a camp of white men near at hand, but which had not been discovered by the enemy.

At Asher's Station, two miles and a half from where Gallatin now stands, some white men were sleeping in a cabin; the Indians crept up at break of day, and fired, killing one man, whom they scalped. They also wounded another, Phillips, and captured several horses. With these, they went off in the direction of Bledsoe's Lick, when they were unexpectedly met by Alexander Buchanan, James Manifee, William Ellis, Alexander Thompson, and other hunters, returning to the Bluff. Buchanan killed one Indian; another was wounded, and the whole party dispersed, leaving, in their flight, the horses taken from Spencer and Philips.

In May of this year, Freeland's Station was visited by the Indians; one man, D. Lariman, was killed, and his head cut off. The whites pursued the retreating savages to the neighborhood of Duck River, near the place since known as Gordon's Ferry, where they came in hearing of them preparing their campfires. The party of white men immediately dismounted, and marched upon the Indian camp, which was found deserted; the enemy escaped. Of the pursuers, who numbered about twenty, the names only of four are known; Alexander Buchanan, John Brock, William Mann, and Capt. James Robertson. This was the first military excursion in that direction, and reflects great credit upon the adventure and gallantry of those who made it. As it was bloodless, the enemy was not deterred from repeating their inroads and aggressions upon the feeble settlements on the Cumberland, and, in a short time after, Isaac Lefevre was killed near the fort on the Bluff, at the spot where Nathan Ewing, Esq., since lived. Solomon Philips went out, about the same time, to the place since called Cros's Old Field, and was shot at, and wounded, by the Indians. He survived till he reached the fort, but soon died. Samuel Murray, who was with him in the field, was shot dead. Near the mound, south of where the steam-mill since stood, Bartlett Renfroe was killed, and John Maxwell and John Kendrick were taken prisoners.

It has been already mentioned, that some of the emigrants that had come in boats down the Tennessee, had stopped at Red River, with the intention of there forming a settlement. Amongst these, were several families of the name of Renfroe, and their connexions, Nathan and Solomon Turpin. In June or July, their settlement was attacked by a party of Choctaws and Chickasaw Indians; Nathan Turpin and another man were killed at the station. The residue were forced to withdraw to the stronger settlement at the Bluff. The Renfroes took charge of the women and children, and conducted them in safely. They afterwards, in company with others from the Bluff, went to the station on Red River, got quiet possession of some property they had left there, and were upon their return march. At night they encamped about two miles north of Sycamore, at a creek, since called Battle Creek. In the morning, Joseph Renfroe going to the spring, was fired at and instantly killed by the Indians, who lay concealed in the bushes. They then broke in upon the camp, and killed old Mr. Johns and his wife, and all his family. Only one woman, Mrs. Jones, escaped; Henry Ramsey, a bold and intrepid man, who had gone from the Bluff, took her off, and brought her in safety to the station. Eleven or twelve others, there at the time of the attack, were all killed; the Indians, taking possession of the horses and other property, went off towards the south.

The ostensible ground of these hostilities by the Chickasaws, was the erection, by Gen. George Rogers Clarke, of Fort Jefferson, eighteen miles below the mouth of the Ohio, and on the east side of the Mississippi. All the territory west of the Tennessee, the Chicasaws pretended to hold by an indisputed claim. Offended at Clarke's intrusion upon their lands, these savages, till then neutral, became the allies of the British nation, and were so at the time this mischief was perpetrated. In 1782, Capt. Robertson made peace with them.

[1780] In the summer of this year, Philip Catron, riding from Freeland's Station to the Bluff, was fired on by the Indians, at the place since occupied by Ephraim Foster, Esq. He was wounded in the breast, so that he spit blood, but he recovered. About the same time, as Capt. John Caffrey and Daniel Williams were rising the bank, in going towards the Bluff, they were fired upon and wounded. They reached the station.

In the fall of this year, the Indians depredated further upon the settlers, by stealing horses from the Bluff. Leiper, with fifteen men, pursued and overtook them on the south side of Harper, near where Ellison formerly lived. They were encamped at night, and the evening was wet. Leiper and his men fired upon them, wounded one, regained their horses and all their baggage, and returned.

Nearly at the same time, Col. John Donaldson had gone up the Cumberland to the Clover Bottom, with two boats, for the purpose of bringing to the Bluff the corn which he and others had raised there the preceding summer. They had laden the boats with the corn, and had proceeded a small distance down the river, when the Colonel, recollecting that he had forgotten to gather some cotton which had been planted at the lower end of the field, asked the men in the other boat to put to bank, for the purpose of picking out a part of it. They urged that it was growing late, and that they ought to go on. He waived the exercise of his autho.ity, and had scarcely landed his own boat, when his companions in the other were suddenly attacked by a party of Indians, who lay in ambush to intercept the boats on their return. The fire of the Indians was fatal. All were killed except a free negro and one white man, who swam to shore, and wandered many days in the woods before he reached the Bluff. The next morning after the defeat, the people at the Station found the boat floating in the river. It was brought to the shore, and a dead man was in it. In this affair, Abel Gower, Sr., and Abel Gower, Jr., and John Robertson, son of Capt. Robertson, were killed. Some others were wounded and taken prisoners. Col. Donaldson escaped to Mansco's Station.

The only one of the settlers who died, the first year a natural death, was Robert Gilkey.

Michael Stoner, this year, discovered Stoner's Lick and Stoner's Creek.

The woods abounded in game, and the hunters procured a full supply of meat for the inhabitants by killing bears, buffalo and deer. A party of twenty men went up the Cany Fork as high as Flinn's Creek, and returned in canoes with their meat, during the winter. In their hunting excursion they killed one hundred and five bears, seventy-five buffalo, and more than eighty deer. This source of supply furnished most of the families at the Bluff with meat. A freshet, in July, had destroyed most of the corn on the lowlands and islands, and many suffered the want of bread. The scarcity of this article, and the multiplied disasters and dangers which every moment threatened the settlements with destruction, at length disheartened some of the inhabitants. A considerable part of them moved to Kentucky and Illinois. The severity of the winter and the want of horses, put a stop to this emigration, and all the remaining inhabitants collected themselves together into two stations—the Bluff and Freeland's.

[1781] Forty or fifty Indians, at the still hour of midnight, January 15th, of this year, made an attack on Freeland's Station. Capt. James Robertson had, the evening before, returned from the Kentucky settlements. Whilst on his journey through the intervening wilderness, he had accustomed himself to more vigilance than the residents of the fort felt it necessary, in their fancied security, to exercise. He was the first to hear the noise which the cautious savages made in opening the gate. He arose and alarmed the men in the station. But the Indians had effected an entrance. The cry of *Indians*, brought Major Lucas out of bed; he was shot. The alarm having become general, the Indians retreated through the gate, but fired in the port-holes through the house in which Major Lucas lived. In this house a negro of Capt. Robertson was shot. These were the only fatal shots; though not less than five hundred were fired into that house; it was the only one in which the port-holes were not filled up with mud. The whites numbered only eleven, but they made good use of the advantage they possessed in the other houses in the fort. Capt. Robertson shot an Indian. The whole body of them soon after retreated. The moon shone bright, otherwise this attack would probably have succeeded, as the fort was once in possession of the Indians. They had found means to loosen the chain on the inside, which confined the gate, and they were also superior in numbers.

After this repulse, the Indians received reinforcements from the Cherokee nation. They burnt up every thing before them, immense quantities of corn and other produce, as well as the houses and fences, and the unoccupied stations of the whites. The alarm became general. All who could get to the Bluff or Eaton's Station, did so, but many never saw their comrades in those places; some were killed sleeping; some were awakened only to be apprised that their last moment was come; some were killed in the noon-day, when not suspecting danger; death seemed ready to embrace the whole of the adventurers. In the morning when Mansco's Lick Station was broken up, two men who had slept a little later than their companions, were shot by two guns pointed through a port-hole by the Indians. These were David Goin and Patrick Quigley. Many of the terrified settlers moved to Kentucky, or went down the river. It is strange that all did not go out of the way of impending danger. Heroism was then an attribute even with the gentler sex. Mrs. Dunham sent a small girl out of the fort, to bring in something she wanted, and the Indians being there, took hold of the child and scalped, without killing her. The mother hearing the cries of the child, advanced towards the place where she was, and was shot by the Indians and wounded dangerously. She and the daughter lived many years afterwards.

 Late in March, of this year, Col. Samuel Barton, passing near the head of the branch which extends from the stone bridge, was fired upon by Indians in ambush, and wounded in the wrist. He ran with the blood streaming from the wound, followed by a warrior in close pursuit. They were seen from the fort, and Martin, one of the soldiers in it, ran out to meet and assist his comrade. The pursuing Indian retreated.

On the second day of April, in this year, a desperate attempt was made by the Indians to take the fort and station at the Bluff. A numerous body of Cherokee warriors came there in the night and lay around in ambush. Next morning three of them came in sight, and fired at the fort on the Bluff and immediately retreated. Nineteen horsemen in the fort at once mounted their horses and followed them. When they came to the branch, over which the stone bridge has since been built, they discovered Indians in the creek and in the thickets near it. These arose from their places of concealment and fired upon the horsemen. The latter dismounted to give them battle, and returned their fire with great alacrity. Another party of the enemy lay concealed in the wild brush and cedars, near the place where Mr. De Mumbrune's house stood in 1821, ready to rush into the fort, in rear of the combatants. The horses ran back to the fort—the horsemen being left on foot. To guard against the expected assault from the Indians against those in the fort, its gates were closed, and preparations made for defence. In the meantime, the battle raged without. Peter Gill, Alexander Buchanan, George Kennedy, Zachariah White and Capt. Leiper, were killed on the spot. James Manifee and Joseph Moonshaw, and others, were wounded before they could reach the fort. At the place where the stone house of Cross was afterwards built, Isaac Lucas had his thigh broken by a ball. His comrades had gotten within the fort, and the Indians rushed upon him to take his scalp. One of them running towards him, and being at a short distance from the supposed victim of his barbarous revenge, was fired upon and shot through the body by Lucas, who, with his rifle well charged, was lying unable to rise from the ground. The Indian died instantly. The people in the fort, in order to save Lucas, kept up a brisk and warm fire upon those parties of the assailants who attempted to get to him, and finally succeeded in driving them off. Lucas was taken and brought into the fort by his own people.

Amongst those who escaped towards the fort, was Edward Swanson, who was so closely pursued by an Indian warrior as to be overtaken by him. The Indian punched him with the muzzle of his gun, and pulled trigger, when the gun snapped. Swanson laid hold of the muzzle, and wringing the lock to one side, spilled the priming from the pan. The Indian looked into the pan, and finding no powder in it, struck him with the gun barrel, the muzzle foremost; the stroke not bringing him to the ground, the Indian clubbed his gun, and striking Swanson with it near the lock, knocked him down. At this moment John Buchanan, Sr., father of the late Major Buchanan, seeing the certain death that impended his comrade, gallantly rushed from the fort to the rescue of Swanson. Coming near enough to fire, he discharged his rifle at the Indian, who, gritting his teeth, on receiving its contents, retired to a stump near at hand. Buchanan brought off Swanson, and they both got into the fort without further injury. From the stump to which the wounded warrior retired, was found, after the Indian forces had withdrawn, a trail, made by a body dragged along upon the ground, much marked with blood.

When the Indians fired upon the horsemen at the branch, the party of them lying in ambush at Demumbrune's, rose and marched towards the river, forming a line between the combatants and the fort. In the meantime, when the firing between the dismounted horsemen and the enemy had commenced, the horses took fright, and ran in full speed on the south side of the Indian line towards the French Lick, passing by the fort on the Bluff. Seeing this, a number of Indians in the line, eager to get possession of the horses, left their ranks and went in pursuit of them. At this instant the dogs in the fort, seeing the confusion, and hearing the firing, ran towards the branch, and came to that part of the Indian line that remained yet unbroken, and having been trained to hostilities against Indians, made a most furious onset upon them, and disabled them from doing anything more than defending themselves. Whilst thus engaged, the whites passed near them through the interval in the Indian line made by those who had gone from it in pursuit of the horses. Had it not been for these fortunate circumstances, the white men could never have succeeded in reaching the fort through the Indian line which had taken post between it and them. Such of the nineteen as survived, would have had to break through the line, their own guns being empty, whilst those of the Indians were well charged.

This attack was well planned by the Indians, and was carried on with some spirit. At length they retired, leaving upon the field the dead Indian killed by Lucas; another was found buried on the east side of the creek, in a hollow, north of the place since occupied by Mr. Hume. Many of the Indians were seen hopping with lame feet or legs, and otherwise wounded. Their loss could never be ascertained. It must have been considerable. They got nineteen horses, saddles, bridles and blankets, and could easily remove their dead and wounded.

On the night of the same day in which this affair took place, another party of Indians, who had not come up in time to be present at the battle, marched to the ground since occupied by Poyzer's and Condon's houses and lots, and fired some time upon the fort. A swivel, charged with small rocks and pieces of pots, was discharged at them. They immediately withdrew.

In the summer of this year, William Hood was

killed by a party of Indians, on the outside of the fort, at Freeland's Station. They did not, at this time, attack the station. Between that place and the French Lick, about the same time, they killed old Peter Renfroe, and withdrew. In the fall, Timothy Terril, from North Carolina, was killed.

As Jacob Freeland was hunting on Stoner's Lick Creek, at the place where John Castleman since lived, he was killed by the Indians. There, also, at another time, they killed Joseph Castleman. Jacob Castleman soon after, going in the woods to hunt, was surprised and killed.

[1782.] Like atrocities marked the spring of this year. At the French Lick, three persons were fired upon by a party of Indians. John Tucker and Joseph Hendricks were wounded, and being pursued till in sight of the fort, they were rescued and their pursuers repulsed. The third, David Hood, the Indians shot down, scalped and trampled upon him, believing him dead, they left him and gave chase to his wounded comrades. Hood, supposing the Indians were gone, wounded and scalped as he was, got up softly, and began to walk towards the fort at the Bluff. To his mortification and surprise, he saw, standing upon the bank of the creek before him, the same Indians who had wounded him, making sport of his misfortunes and mistake. They then fell on him again, and inflicting other apparently mortal wounds, left him. He fell into a brush-heap in the snow, and next morning, search being made by the whites, he was found by his blood, and being taken home, was placed in an out-house as a dead man. To the surprise of all, he revived, and after some time recovered, and lived many years.

The first mill erected was near Eaton's Station, on the farm since occupied by Mr. Talbot. It was the property of James Wells, Esq.; the next, by Colonel George Mansco; the third, by Capt. Frederick Stump, on White's Creek; the fourth, by David Ronfifer, on the same creek; and the next, by Major J. Buchanan.

After their unsuccessful attempt against the Bluff, in 1781, the Indians continued occasional irruptions and depredations throughout the forming settlements on Cumberland. In that year little corn was raised. The scarcity of grain compelled the settlers to plant more largely, and raise more grain in 1782, and to procure subsistance by hunting. In both these pursuits, many became victims to the stratagem and cruelty of their savage enemy.

A settlement had been begun at Kilgore's Station, on the north side of the Cumberland, on Red River. At this place Samuel Martin and Isaac Johnston, returning to the Bluff, were fired upon by the Indians. They took Martin prisoner, and carried him into the Creek nation. He remained there nearly a year, and came home elegantly dressed, with two valuable horses and silver spurs. It was said, afterwards, that he had concerted with the Indians the time and place of the attack made by them, and that he was a sharer in the plunder. Isaac Johnston escaped and came home.

Of the other settlers at Kilgore's, were two young men named Mason, Moses Malding, Ambrose Malding, Josiah Hoskins, Jesse Simons, and others. The two young men, Mason, had gone to Clay Lick, and had posted themselves in a secret place to watch for deer. Whilst they were there thus situated, seven Indians came to the Lick; the lads took good aim, fired upon and killed two Indians, and then ran with all speed to the fort, where, being joined by three of the garrison, they returned to the Lick, found and scalped the dead Indians, and returned. That night John and Ephraim Peyton, on their way to Kentucky, called in and remained all night at the fort. During the night all the horses that were there were stolen. In the morning pursuit was made, and the Indians were overtaken in the evening, at a creek, since called Peyton's Creek. They were fired upon. One was killed and the rest of them fled, leaving the stolen horses to their owners. The pursuers returned that night, in the direction of the fort, and encamped, and were progressing, next morning, on their way. In the meantime, the Indians, by a circuitous route, had got between them and the station, and when the whites came near enough, fired upon them, killing one of the Mason, and Josiah Hoskins, and taking some spoil. The Indians then retreated. Discouraged by these daring depredations, the people at Kilgore's Station broke up their establishment and joined those at the Bluff.

In this year, also, George Aspie was killed, on Drake's Creek, by the Indians, and Thomas Spencer wounded. In the fall William McMurray was killed near Winchester's Mill, on Bledsoe's Creek, and General Smith was wounded. Noah Trammel was killed on Goose Creek. Malden's Station, on Red River, was broken up and abandoned.

Such were the difficulties and dangers that accompanied the infancy of the Cumberland settlements, that, from necessity, it became a custom of the country for one or two persons to stand as watchmen or sentinels, whilst others labored in the field; and even whilst one went to a spring to drink, another stood on the watch, with his rifle ready to protect him, by shooting a creeping Indian, or one rising from the thickets of canes and brush that covered him from view; and wherever four or five were assembled together at a spring, or other place, where business required them to be, they held their guns in their hands, and with their backs turned to each other, one faced the north, another the south, another the west —watching, in all directions, for a lurking or creeping enemy. Whilst the people at the Bluff were so much harrassed and galled by the Indians that they could not plant nor cultivate their corn-fields, a proposition was made, in a council of the inhabitants, to break up the settlements and go off. Captain Robertson pertinaciously resisted this proposition. It was then impossible to reach Kentucky; the Indians were in force upon all the roads and passages which led to it; for the same reason, it was also impossible, and equally impracticable, to remove to the settlements on Holston. No other means of escape remained, but that of going down the river in boats, and making good their retreat to the Illinois. And even to this plan, great obstacles were opposed; for how was the wood to be obtained, with which to make the boats? The Indians were, every day, in the skirts of the Bluff, lying concealed among the shrubs and cedar trees, ready to inflict death upon whoever should attempt to go to the woods. These difficulties were all stated by Captain Robertson. He held out the dangers attendant upon the attempt, on the one hand; the fine country they were on the point of possessing, on the other. To these he added, the probability of new acquisitions of numbers from the older settlements, and the certainty of being able, by careful attention to circumstances, to defend and support themselves till succor could arrive. At length, the parental advice and authority of Robertson prevailed. He finally succeeded in quieting the apprehensions of his co-colonists; and they gradually relinquished the design of evacuating the positions they occupied, now somewhat hallowed to them by the recollection of past dangers, endured toils, difficulties overcome, and triumphs achieved.

The expectations of Captain Robertson were, in part, soon realized. The revolutionary war was ended; an abatement of Indian hostility soon followed; and additional emigrants from North Carolina and other States, gave renewed strength and animation and permanence to his settlement.

[1783.] But, notwithstanding these favorable circumstances, offering, as they did, some alleviation of the suffering endured on Cumberland, still, in 1783, the offensive operations of the Indians were occasionally continued. One of the guard who came to the Bluff with the Commissioners from North Carolina, Roger Top, was killed at the place where Mr. Deaderick has since lived. At the same time and place, Roger Glass was wounded. Within two days after these acts of hostility, a settler, passing the place where the stone bridge now is, was shot at and wounded by the Indians. He succeeded in reaching the fort, but died soon afterwards.

The Chickasaws, early in 1783, assembled in the vicinity of Nashville, at Robertson's Station, where a treaty was concluded, ceding and relinquishing to

North Carolina a region of country extending nearly forty miles south of Cumberland River, to the ridge dividing the tributaries of that stream from those of Duck and Elk.*

The policy of Spain, at this time, was, to secure the good feelings, if not the aid, af the southern Indians. The agents of that power invited those tribes to meet and hold conferences with them, at the Walnut Hills. From these conferences they returned, as was believed, with dispositions less amicable to the new settlements on the Cumberland. No large body of them invaded that country, but small parties of Indians were constantly waylaying the paths and surrounding the corn-fields of the emigrants. Such of them as were exploring the country, and making locations, were closely watched, and some of them killed. Ireson and Barnette, on a surveying excursion, were shot down and killed. On Richland Creek, near what has since been the plantation of Mr. Irwin, William Daniel, Joseph Dunham, Joshua Norrington, and Joel Mills, were all killed; and in a path leading from Dunham's Fort to Armstrong's, at the head of the same creek, where Castleman since lived, a soldier was killed as he passed from one fort to the other.

At Armstrong's Fort, as Patsy, the daughter of Mr. Rains, was riding on horseback, with a young woman Betsy Williams, behind her, they were fired upon by

---
*Monette, ii, 268

the Indians, and the latter killed; the former escaped. A short time afterwards, near the same place, Joseph Noland escaped; and during the same summer, a son of Thomas Noland; and during the fall, the old man, himself, were also killed near this same place. About the same time, the Indians killed the father of Betsey Williams, above mentioned.

Buchanan's Station was upon Mill Creek, five miles from the Bluff, not far from the farm at the present time owned by A. R. Crozier, Esq., on the turnpike leading from Nashville to Lebanon. There the Indians, in this year, killed Samuel Buchanan, William Mulherrin and three others, who was guarding the station. Going from the Bluff to Kentucky, William Overall was killed, and Joshua Thomas mortally wounded. The Indians having stolen horses from the Bluff, Captain William Pruett raised twenty men pursued them to Richland Creek of Elk River, overtook them, and recaptured the horses on the waters of Big Creek. They fired upon, but did not kill any of the Indians. As they returned, they encamped near a creek on the north side of Duck River. As they began their march next morning, they were fired upon by the Indians in their rear. Moses Brown killed in a cane-brake, and the ground being unfavorable, the whites retreated a mile and a half to more open ground, and there halted and formed. The Indians came up and an engagement ensued. Captain Pruett and Daniel Johnson were shot down, and Morris Shine was wounded. Being overpowered, the survivors of the party made good their escape to the Bluff, with the loss of their recaptured horses.

These repeated aggressions and depredations upon the lives and property of the settlers, were the more pertinaciously renewed and persisted in, from the fact that North Carolina had, in April of this year, appropriated the lands hitherto claimed by the Chickasaws and Cherokees, except those which, by the same act, were allowed to them for their hunting grounds. This unceremonious intrusion upon their supposed rights, together with the machinations of the agents of Spain, had the effect to exasperate their hostility to the settlements of the whites now beginning to expand and acquire permanence, by the additional strength of other emigrants from a different direction. Turnbull, a trader, came from Natchez with horses and skins procured in the Chickasaw nation. From the same place, Absalom Hooper, Thomas James, Philip Alston, James Drumgold, James Cole, James Donaldson and others, also arrived. A station was this year established by Samuel Hays on Stone's River.

[1784.] Constantly harrassed and alarmed by the continued recurrence of Indian hostility against his colony, Col. Robertson could no longer resist the conviction, that his savage neighbors on the south were instigated in their unfriendly conduct to the people on Cumberland by some foreign influence, and he suspected that influence might be from the agents of Spain. He entered into correspondence with one of them, Mr. Portell, assuring him of a disposition on the part of his countrymen to maintain with the Spanish colonists the most friendly relations. Mr. Portell, in reply, expressed his gratitude for the amicable behavior of the Cumberland people, and promised to maintain the best relations on his side, and expressed a wish to be useful to the Colonel and his countrymen. Still, incursions for the purpose of murder and plunder, continued to be made by the Indians. Early in this year, Philip Trammel and Philip Mason were killed. As one amongst a thousand instances of the unequalled fortitude and gallantry of the first settlers, a recitation is here given of the conflict in which they ended their existence. These two men had killed a dear at the head of White's Creek, and were skinning it. The Indians stole up to the place and fired upon them. They wounded Mason and carried off the venison. Trammel got assistance from Eaton's Station, and followed the Indians. He came up with them; they fought, and he killed two of them. The Indians being reinforced, and Mason having received a second and mortal wound, the whites were once more obliged to retreat. Trammel found some other white men in the woods, and induced them to go back with him to the place where the Indians were. They found the latter, and immediately renewed the fight. They killed three Indians, and fought till both parties were tired. Trammel and Josiah Hoskins, enthusiastically courageous, and determined to make the enemy yield the palm of victory, gallantly precipitated themselves into the midst of the retreating Indians, where they fell by the hands of the foe. The rest of the white men maintained their ground until both parties were exhausted and willing to rest from their martial labors.

Another spirited affair, scarcely less heroic, deserves also to be specially mentioned. Aspie, Andrew Lucas, Thomas S. Spencer and Johnston, had left the Bluff on horseback on a hunting tour. They had reached the head-waters of Drake's Creek, where their horses had stopped to drink. At this moment a party of Indians fired upon them. Lucas was shot through the neck and through the mouth. He, however, dismounted with the rest, but in attempting to fire, the blood gushed from his mouth and wet his priming; perceiving this, he crawled into a bunch of briers. Aspie, as he alighted from his horse, received a bullet which broke his thigh; but he still fought heroically. Johnston and Spencer acquitted themselves with incomparable gallantry, but were obliged to give way, and to leave Aspie to his fate, though he entreated them earnestly not to forsake him. The Indians killed and scalped Aspie, but did not find

Lucas, who shortly afterwards returned to his friends. Spencer, in the heat of the engagement, was shot, but the ball split on the bone and his life was spared. The whole Aspie family were superlatively brave. A brother had been previously killed in the battle at the Bluff. · When he first fell, he placed himself in a position to reach a loaded gun, with which he shot an Indian running up to scalp him.

In tnis year also, Cornelius Riddle was shot by the Indians, near Buchanan's Station. He had killed two turkeys, and hanging them upon a bush, had gone off into the woods to hunt for more. The Indians hearing the report of his gun, came to the place, and finding the turkeys, lay in ambush where they were, and on Riddle's coming to take them away, they fired upon and killed him.

In the year 1785, Moses Brown was killed, near the place on Richland Creek, afterwards occupied by Jesse Wharton, Esq., and then known as Brown's Station. Col. Robertson and Col. Weakley had gone, with Edmond Hickman, a Surveyor, to survey entered lands on Piny River. The Indians came upon them suddenly, and killed Hickman. The same year they killed a man living with William Stuart, on the plantation where Judge Haywood afterwards lived.

Notwithstanding these daring acts of hostillty, the number of inhabitants steadily increased. James

Harrison, William Hall and W. Gibson, settled this year above Bledsoe's Lick, and Charles Morgan established a station on the west side of Bledsoe's Creek, five miles from the Lick. The Indians killed Peter Barnett and David Steele, below Clarksville, on the waters of Blooming Grove. They also wounded Wm. Crutcher and went off, leaving a knife sticking in him; he recovered.

On the second day of March, John Peyton, a Surveyor, Ephraim Peyton, Thomas Pugh and John Frazier, had commenced their survey upon a creek, since called Defeated Creek, on the north side of Cumberland, in what is now Smith county, and had made a camp. While they were sleeping around the camp about midnight, a great number of Cherokee Indians surrounded and fired upon them. All but one of them were wounded, but they ran through the Indian line, made their escape and got home, losing their horses, compass, chain, blankets, saddles and bridles. The Indians retreated immediately to their towns, and were not overtaken.

[1786] The Commissioners of the United States, Benjamin Hawkins, Andrew Pickens, and Joseph Martin, concluded a treaty with the Chckasaw Commissioners, Piomingo, head warrior and first minister, Mingatushka, one of the leading chiefs, and Latopoia, first beloved man of that nation, at Hopewell, January 10, 1786. The boundary of the lands allotted to the Chickasaw nation to live and hunt on,

" Began on the ridge that divides the waters running into the Cumberland from those running into the Tennessee, at a point in a line to be run north-east, which shall strike the Tennessee at the mouth of Duck River; thence running westerly along the said ridge till it shall strike the Ohio; thence down the southern bank thereof to the Mississippi; thence down the Choctaw line of Natchez District; thence along the said line, or the line of the district, eastwardly as far as the Chickasaws claimed, and lived and hunted on, the twenty-ninth of November, one thousand seven hundred and eighty-two. Thence the said boundary eastwardly shall be the lands alloted to the Choctaws and Cherokees, to live and hunt on, and the lands at present in possession of the Creeks, saving and reserving for the establishment of a trading post, a tract of land, to be laid out at the lower point of the Muscle Shoals, at the mouth of Ocochappo."

Monette says, that the Chickasaws, by his treaty, ratified and confirmed that made in 1783, with Donaldson and Martin, Commissioners of North Carolina. This treaty encouraged emigration to Cumberland.

[1787] The settlements were now becoming stronger by annual arrivals of emigrants, but had not expanded much, except in the direction towards Red River.

There the new settlers underwent the usual initiation from Indian outrage and aggression. Hendrick's Station, on Station Camp Creek, was assaulted in the night; the house, in which were Mr. and Mrs. Price and their children, was broken into, the parents were killed and their children badly wounded. A boy named Baird, was killed in the day time, and several horses were stolen. Near the Locust-land, where Gen. Hall since lived, above Bledsoe's Lick, the Indians killed William Hall and his son Richard, and another man. In May, the Indians came to Richland Creek, and in daylight killed Mark Robertson, near the place where Robertson's mill was since erected. He was a brother of Col. Robertson, and was returning from his house.

During the summer, the Indians came to Drake's Creek, where William Montgomery lived, shot down and scalped his son, and wounded John Allen. In the same neighborhood they killed Mr. Morgan, Sen., and were pursued by a party of white men under the command of George Winchester, who followed on their trail. Another party, commanded by Captain William Martin, also followed them by a nearer route, and not having found their trail, encamped near it. The other party, on the same night, came on the trail, and seeing the camp of Martin, fired into it and killed William Ridley, the son of George Ridley, late of Davidson county.

Considerable delay occurred before Evans's battalion could be recruited, equipped, provided with supplies, and sent forward to Cumberland, as provided for by the Assembly of North Carolina. Impatient of this delay, Col. Bledsoe asks permission of Gov. Caswell to carry an expedition against the Chickamaugas. His letter is dated from Kentucky, whither he and Col. Robertson had gone, to procure additional forces, with which to chastise the enemy.

"KENTUCKY, June 1st, 1887.

"*Dear Sir:*—At this place I received accounts from Cumberland, that since I last did myself the pleasure of addressing you, three persons have been killed at that place, within about seven miles of Nashville; and there is scarcely a day, that the Indians do not steal horses in either Sumner or Davidson counties; and I am informed, the people are exceedingly dispirited, having had accounts that several northern tribes, in conjunction with the Creek nation, have determined the destruction of that defenceless country, this summer; and their hopes seem blasted, as to Major Evans's assistance. Col. Robertson has lately been to this country to get some assistance to carry on a campaign against the Chickamauga towns, and got some assurance from the several officers. The time appointed for the rendezvous, was fixed to the 15th instant, but, finding the men cannot be drawn out at that season of the year, I have thought it my duty to ask your advice in the matter; whether, or not, we shall have leave of government to carry on such a campaign, if we can make ourselves able, with the assistance of our friends, the Virginians, as they promised us, immediately after harvest."

Soon after the date of Col. Bledsoe's letter, that officer and Col. Robertson addressed Gov. Caswell, jointly, under date :

"CUMBERLAND, June 12th, 1787.

"*Dear Sir.*—Nothing but the distress of a bleeding country could induce us to trouble you on so disagreeable a subject. We enclose you a list of the killed in this quarter, since our departure from this country to the Assembly; this, with the numbers wounded, the vast numbers of horses stolen from the inhabitants, has, in a degree, flagged the spirits of the people: A report is now here, and has prevailed throughout this country, and we are induced to believe it is true, that the Spaniards are doing all they can to encourage the several savage tribes to war against the Americans. It is certain, the Chickasaws inform us, that Spanish traders offer a reward for scalps of the Americans. A disorderly set of French and Spanish traders are continually on the Tennessee, that, we actually fear, are a great means of encouraging the Indians to do us much mischief. We should wish to take some measure to remove these disorderly traders from the Tennessee, and wish your Excellency's advice in the matter."

At length, the Indian atrocities becoming so bold and frequent, it appeared necessary, for the protection and defence of the settlements, that offensive operations should be carried on against the Indians in their own towns. One hundred and thirty men, from the different settlements on Cumberland, volunteered for that purpose, and assembled at the house of Col. Robertson. Of this force he took the command, assisted by Col. Robert Hayes and Col. James Ford, and marched for the Indian village, Coldwater, with two Chickasaws as pilots. They crossed at the mouth of South Harper; thence they went a direct course to the mouth of Turnbull's Creek, and up that stream to its head; thence to Lick Creek, of Duck River; thence down that creek seven or eight miles, leaving the creek to the right hand; thence to an old and very large Lick; thence to Duck River, where the old Chickasaw trace crossed it; thence, leaving the trace to the right hand, they went to the head of Swan Creek; thence to a creek then called Blue Water, running into the Tennessee River, about a mile and a half above the lower end of the Muscle Shoals. When within ten miles of these rapids, they heard the roaring of the falls. One of the Indian guides, with several of the most active soldiers, was ordered to go to the river. These, about midnight, returned, saying the river was too distant for them to reach that night and return to camp. In the morning, they pursued the same course they had done the day before. At 12 o'clock, they struck the river at the lower end of the Muscle Shoals, where it is said the road now crosses, and concealed themselves in the woods till night. On the north side of the river they discovered, on a bluff, a plain path leading along the river, which seemed to be much travelled; and on the south side, opposite to them, were seen several Indian cabins or lodges. Several of the soldiers went down secretly, took their station under the bank, and concealed themselves under the cane, to observe what could be seen on the other side. They had not long remained in their place of concealment, when they saw some Indians reconnoitering and evidently looking out for the troops of Col. Robertson. In doing this, they passed into an island near the south bank of the river, where they entered a canoe, and came half way over the stream. Not being able to see any of the invaders, the Indians returned to the island where they had started from, and fastened the canoe.

When they left the river, Captain Rains was sent with fifteen men up the path, along the north bank, with orders from Col. Robertson to capture an Indian, if possible, alive. He executed the order, but did not see an Indian. He went nearly to the mouth of Bluewater Creek, when about sunset he was recalled, having made no discoveries. It was determined to cross the river that night, and the soldiers, who had watched the movements of the Indians, swam over the river and went up to the cabins, but they found not a single living being in the village. They then untied the canoe and returned in it to the north bank. It was found to be a very large one, but old and having a hole in its bottom. This the men contrived to stop with their shirts. Into this frail and leaky barque, forty men, with their fire-arms, entered. They started from the shore, and the canoe sprang a leak and began to sink. Jumping into the water, the men swam back with the canoe to the northern bank. In these operations, some noise was necessarily made, and considrable time consumed, and the embarkation of the troops was delayed till daylight. With a piece of linn bark the hole in the canoe was at length covered, and forty or fifty men crossed over in it, and took possession of the bank on the south side. The remainder of the troops swam over with the horses. Having all crossed the river in safety, attention was paid to drying their clothes and equipments. A rain came on and forced the men into the cabins. After the clouds cleared away, the troops mounted, and seeing a well beaten path, leading from the river out into the barrens, in a western direction, they dashed into it and followed it briskly. At the distance of five or six miles they came to corn fields, and a mile or two further they came to Coldwater Creek. This most of the troops crossed by a path so narrow that a single shorse could only pass it up the bank. On the the other side of the creek was a number of cabins, built upon the low grounds, which extended to the river about three hundred yards below. The people of the town were surprised by its sudden and unexpected invasion, and fled precipitately to their boats at the river, and were closely pursued by such of the men as had crossed the creek. Captain Rains had remained on its other side, with Benjamin Castleman, William Loggins, William Steele and Martin Duncan, and seeing the retreat and flight of the enemy, went down the east side of the creek to intercept them. The retreating Indians, as they ran down on the other side, and had their attention drawn to those who pursued them on the same side of the creek, crossed over and came to the spot where Captain Rains and his men were, and were fired upon, while looking back at their pursuers, and not perceiving the snare into which they had fallen. Three of them dropped down dead. Three French traders and a white woman, who had got into a boat and would not surrender, but mixed with the Indians and seemed determined to partake of their fate, whatever it might be, were killed by the troops. They wounded and took prisoner the principal trader and owner of the goods, and five or six other Frenchmen, who lived there as traders. These had in the town stores of taffia, sugar, coffee, cloths, blankets, Indian wares of all sorts, salt, shot, Indian paints, knives, powder, tomahawks, tobacco and other articles, suitable for Indian commerce. The troops killed many of the Indians after they had got into the boats, and gave them so hot and deadly a fire from the bank of the river, that they were forced to jump into water, and were shot whilst in it, until, as the Chickasaws afterwards informed them, twenty-six of the Creek warriors were killed in the river. The troops immediately afterwards collected all the boats that were upon the river, and brought them up the creek, opposite the town, and placed a guard over them. Each of the Indian guides was, next morning, presented with a horse, a gun, and as many blankets and clothes as the horses could carry, as their portion of the spoils, and despatched to their homes. The name of one of them was Toka, a chief.

After the departure of the Chickasaw guides, the troops buried the white men and the women killed in the engagement of the day before, set fire and burned up the town, and destroyed the domestic animals that were found in and around it. The goods of the traders had been removed from the stores, and with the prisoners, were now put into three or four boats, under the charge of Jonathan Denton, Benjamin Drake, and John and Moses Eskridge, to navigate them.

They were directed to descend the Tennessee to some convenient point on its southern shore, where they were to meet the mounted troops, and assist them in crossing. At the time the boats started down the river, the horsemen began their march by land, but being without pilots, and entirely unacquainted with the windings of the stream, they took a course that led them further from it than they intended, into the piny woods, where they encamped. The next day they went to the river, where they saw several persons at a distance on the islands, who proved to be their own boatmen. Neither knew the other till some of the boatmen, nearing the shore, made the agreeable discovery, that the horsemen on the land were their friends. The troops then moved down the river a few miles, and came to a place just above the point of an island, where the descent to the river was easy and convenient for embarkation, and where the bank on the opposite side afforded a safe landing. Here, with the assistance of the boats, they crossed over. The whole command encamped together on the north shore, and found they had not lost a single man, and that not one was wounded. The place at which the crossing was made, is near what has since been known as Colbert's Ferry.

The horsemen, after leaving camp on the Tennessee, marched nearly a north course, till they struck the path leading to the Chickasaw Old Crossing on

Duck river, where they had crossed going out, and pursuing their own trace, returned unmolested to the Bluff.

At the encampment on the Tennessee, the French prisoners were allowed to take all their trunks and wearing apparel, and an equal division was made of the sugar and coffee amongst the troops and prisoners. To the latter was also given a canoe, in which, after bidding farewell, they ascended the river.

The dry goods were ordered, under the care of the same boatmen, to Nashville. Sailing down the river some days, they met other French boats laden with goods, and having on board French traders, who, being greatly rejoiced at seeing their countrymen, as they supposed the Cumberland boatmen to be, returning home, saluted them by firing their guns. The latter, descending the river with their guns charged, came alongside of the French boats, boarded them and captured the boats and crews, and conducted them to a place a few miles below Nashville. There the captors gave the Frenchmen a canoe, and dismissed them with permission to go down the river, which they did.

The spoils taken at Coldwater were brought to Eaton's Station and sold, and the proceeds divided amongst the troops. They returned to Col. Robertson's on the nineteenth day after the commencement

of the expedition at his home. From this place, Col.
Robertson wrote Gov. Caswell under date—

"NASHVILLE, July 2d, 1787.

"*Sir:*—I had the pleasure of receiving your Excellency's letter to Col. Bledsoe and myself, in which you were so obliging as to mention you would render every aid in your power to our country. Never was there a time in which your Excellency's assistance and attention were more necessary than the present. The war being exceedingly hot in the spring, I marched some men near the Chickamaugas; but wishing to avoid an open war, returned without doing them any mischief, leaving a letter containing every offer of peace that could be made on honorable terms; in consequence of which they sent a flag to treat, though I have every reason to doubt their sincerity, as several persons were killed during their stay, and one man at my house, in their sight. They impute the mischief we suffer to the Creeks. A few days after their departure, my brother, Mark Robertson, being killed near my house, I, by the advice of the officers, civil and military, raised about one hundred and thirty men, and followed their tracks, near the lower end of the Muscle Shoals, where some Indians discovered us, fired on our back picket, and alarmed a small town of Cherokees. We found, where we crossed Tennessee, pictures of two scalps, made a few days before; which scalps, we were afterwards informed, were carried into said town by seven Cherokees, who were there when we attacked them. Though they constantly kept out spies, we had the good fortune to cross Tennessee, and go eighteen miles down the river, till in sight of the town, before the Indians discovered us. We made a rapid charge and entirely defeated them. The attack began at the mouth of a large creek; we forced them into the creek and river, and what escaped, either got off in boats or swam the river. About twenty were killed and several wounded. The whole town, as we were afterwards informed by a Frenchman, whom we found there, had been councilling three days, at the instigation of a principal Creek chief, and had unanimously agreed to fight us, if we crossed Tennessee. From what passed at this consultation, I have every reason to believe the Creeks totally averse to peace, notwithstanding they have had no cause of offence. We have been exceedingly particular in giving them no reason to complain. Their force consisted of ten Creeks and thirty-five Cherokee warriors, together with nine Frenchmen, chiefly from Detroit, who had joined the Indians against us. Among the dead was the Creek chief before mentioned, a mischievous Cherokee chief, three Frenchmen and a Frenchwoman, who was killed by accident, in one of the boats. In this action we lost not a single man; but a party of fifty men, who was sent to the mouth of Duck River, was there attacked by a large number of Indians, and we had one man killed and eight wounded. We were piloted by two Chickasaws, in this expedition; their nation seem, on every occasion, our friends, and if it were possible to supply them with trade, at the Chickasaw Bluff, there is no doubt but they and the Choctaws would find full employment for our enemies.

From the constant incursions of the Indians, I have been obliged to keep the militia very much in service on scouts, guards, etc., and have been under the necessity of promising them pay, without which, I am persuaded, the army would have totally broken up, as many have already done. I hope you will approve the promise I have made to the inhabitants. Sumner county seems to be in peace, compared with this; being more out of the range of the Indians. I have not an opportunity of seeing Col. Bledsoe, or I make no doubt he would join me in informing your Excellency that our situation, at present, is deplorable—deprived of raising subsistence, and constantly harrassed with performing military duty, our only hope is in the troops promised us by the General Assembly; but, as yet, we have no news of them. I earnestly beg your Excellency to forward them with all possible expedition. I hope that your Excellency will, by express or otherwise, favor me with an answer."

This spirited invasion of the heart of the Indian country, and the success that had attended the assault against Coldwater, were followed by a short respite from savage aggression. Heretofore, there had not been an hour of safety to any settler on the waters of Cumberland, and offensive measures were adopted and energetically executed. The vengeance so long delayed, had, at length, fallen with most fatal effect upon those who had so frequently provoked it. At Coldwater, Colonel Robertson discovered the sources from which the Indians were supplied with the materials which enabled them to make inroads upon the new settlements; the means by which, and the channels through which, they received them; and the practicable modes of cutting them off, as well as the facility of seizing upon the stores, when deposited in villages near the place of disembarkation. The advantages acquired by his expedition were various and important, and by putting the Indians in danger at home, and making it necessary for them to act on the defensive, near their own villages, had greatly diminished the vigor of their enterprises against the feeble settlements.

These advantages, however, were somewhat counteracted by the unfortunate issue of another expedition, connected, in part, with that so gallantly carried on by Colonel Robertson, and undertaken about the same time, with the view of securing its success.

When the troops started on the campaign to Coldwater, David Hay, of Nashville, had the command of a company there, and determined to carry them, simultaneously, against the enemy, by water; not only to assist their countrymen in the assault upon the Indian villages, but to carry to them provisions and supplies, which, it was apprehended, they might need on their arrival at the Tennessee River, and, particularly, in case of the detention of the horsemen in that neighborhood, for a longer time than was anticipated. Captain Hay and his men descended the river in three boats, and passing around into the Tennessee, had proceeded unmolested up that stream to the mouth of Duck River. When they had reached that stream, the boat commanded by Moses Shelby, entered into it a small distance, for the purpose of examining a canoe, which he observed there, fastened to the bank. A party of Indians had concealed themselves in the canoe and behind the trees, not more than ten or twelve feet from the canoe, and from the boat itself, and poured in a most unexpected fire into the boat. John Top and Hugh Roquering were shot through the body; Edward Hogan through the arm, the ball fracturing the bone; Josiah Renfroe was shot through the head, and killed on the spot. The survivors made great haste to get the boat off, but, having the prow up the small river, and several of the crew being wholly disabled, and some of them greatly dismayed by the sudden fire and destruction which had come upon them, acted in disorder, and with great difficulty got the boat again into the Tennessee, beyond the reach of the Indian guns, before they could reload and fire a second time. Had this movement been executed with less alacrity and despatch, the rash and unadvised act of going to the canoe, would have caused the whole crew to become victims to the stratagem of the Indians. As it was, their artful plot had too well succeded, and the expedition, which promised so much, and thus far had been prosecuted without interruption, was abandoned. Captain Hay returned, with his wounded men, to Nashville, where, alone, surgical and medical assistance could be procured.

The affair at Coldwater, and the capture of the French traders and their goods on the Tennessee, had involved Col. Robertson in a difficulty with a nation then at peace with the United States. That officer deemed it necessary, therefore, to make a written exposition of the causes and motives which led to the campaign which he had conducted, and in which citizens of France had been made to suffer. This communication he addressed to a functionary at the Illinois. He stated in it,

"That for some years past a trade had been carried on by Frenchmen from the Wabash, with the Indians on Tennessee. The trade had been formerly managed by a Mr. Veiz, and while he carried it on the Indians were peaceable towards us; but for two cr three years past, these Indians had been extremely inimical, at all seasons killing our men, women and children, and stealing our horses. He had sufficient evidence of the fact also, that these Indians were excited to war against us by the suggestions of these traders, who both advised them to war and gave them goods for carrying it on. The Chickasaws had told him that they had been offered goods by those traders if they would go to war against us. And one John Rogers declared, that he had seen a Creek fellow have on a pair of arm-bands, which he said were given to him by the French traders, for going to war against our people. Their incursions upon us this spring have been more severe than usual, and I determined to distress them. For this purpose, he stated that he had taken a part of the militia of Davidson county, followed the tracks of one of their scalping parties, who had just been doing murder here, and pursuing them to a town on Tennessee, at the mouth of Coldwater, nad destroyed the town, and killed, as he supposed, about twenty of the Indians. The scalps of two of our people whom they had lately murdered, were found in the town. Some of the French imprudently put themselves in the action, and some of them fell. From that place he sent a party around to the River Cumberland by water. On the

Tennessee they found five Frenchmen, with two boats, having on board goods to trade with those very Indians. The commander of the party captured the boats with the traders, and brought them round to the Cumberland, and gave them their choice, either to come up to the settlement and stand their trial for what they had done, thereby to try and regain their goods, or else they might go home at once without their goods; they chose the latter. The taking of these boats, said Col. Robertson, was without my knowledge or approbation. I am now endeavoring to collect the property which was in them, and I desire the owners to be notified, that if they could make it appear that they were not guilty of a breach of the laws, and did not intend to furnish our enemies with powder, lead and other goods, for our destruction, on applying here at Nashville, they can have their property again. He declared that if those Indians would be peaceable, we should never attempt to deprive them of any trade they could procure. But whilst they continue at war, said he, any traders who furnish them with arms and ammunition, will render themselves very insecure."

The fearless irruption of the troops under Robertson, was followed by a temporary relaxation of Indian hostility. But soon after their route and discomfiture at Coldwater, they collected in small bodies, crossed the Tennessee, and commenced an undistinguishing carnage upon the settlers, of all ages and sexes. One of these was pursued by a small body of white men under Capt. Shannon. The Indians had reached the bank of Tennessee River; some were in their camp, eating, others making preparations to cross to the opposite shore. The former were discovered by Shannon's men, who fired and rushed impetuously upon them. Castleman killed one. Another proving too strong, took Luke Anderson's gun from him, but before he could discharge her, William Pillow, since a Colonel, of Maury county, and the uncle of Gen. Gideon J. Pillow, of the United States Army, shot the Indian and recovered the gun. The remaining Indians, who were without the camp, were commanded by Big Foot, a leading warrior of determined bravery. Believing, from the report of the guns which had been fired, that the number of the assailants was inconsiderable, these resolved to attack the whites, and did so. A terrible conflict ensued. Victory, for some time wavering, at length declared against the Indians. Their leader and five of his followers were killed, the rest raised the yell and disappeared in the bushes.

[1787] Late in July, of this year, two hundred Creek warriors, embodied for the purpose, as they said, of taking satisfaction for three Indians killed in an affair eighteen miles below Chota. Mr. Perrault met and delivered, and expounded to them a letter, written by Col. Robertson, and addressed to their nation. Perrault endeavored to dissuade them from hostilities and to get them to turn back, but his mission was fruitless. They persevered in their march, adding to their rejection of the overtures for peace, a threat, that if their territory should be again invaded, or another Creek should be killed after their present incursion, the whites might expect a merciless war.

Of the battalion ordered to be raised for the protection of Davidson county, Major Evans was appointed to take the command. These troops arrived in Cumberland in successive detachments, accompanying parties of emigrants, that were constantly augmenting the resources and defences of the country. Col. Robertson, to add further to the efficiency of Evans's battalion, was enabled, from the increased strength of the population, to select and detach a certain portion of it to act as patrols or spies. It was their business to go through the woods from the borders of the settlements—in every direction, and to every place where there was an Indian or a buffalo trace—to the crossing places on rivers and creeks, to look after the Indians, and to notice the trails they had made in their marches. At that time canes and weeds grew up so luxuriantly, in all parts of the country, that two or three men, even without horses, could not pass through without leaving a discernible trace, which might be followed with no risk of mistake. Amongst the patrols selected for the performance of this service, was Capt. John Rains. Col. Robertson was led to this choice by the experience he had had in his prowess and diligence. His orders to him had always been executed punctually, promptly, and with a degree of bravery that was never exceeded. An occasion soon offered for the exercise of these eminent qualities. The Indians killed Randall Gentry, not far from the Bluff, at the place where Mr. Foster since lived. About the same time, Curtis Williams and Thomas Fletcher, with his son, were also killed near the mouth of Harper. Captain Rains was ordered to pursue the perpetrators of this mischief. He soon raised sixty men and followed them. Their trace was found and pursuit made; he passed Mill Creek, Big Harper, the Fishing Ford of Duck River, Elk River, at the mouth of Swan Creek, and Flint River. Not being able to overtake the enemy, he left their trace and went westwardly, and struck Mc-Cutchin's trace. Before he reached Elk River, he discovered tracks of Indians going in the direction of Nashville. At the crossing of the river, he came to the camp which they had left the morning before. He went forward six miles and halted, sending forward a few of his men to see that the enemy was not so near as to hear his men forming their encampment. These returned without having seen any of the Indians. Next morning Capt. Rains continued the pursuit, and in the afternoon found the place they had encamped the preceding night. The ground had been cleared of leaves and brush, and upon this the war dance had been celebrated. There were, moreover, evidences of a wary and deliberate invasion for hostile purposes, and of very cautious and watchful progress. The troops, after crossing Duck River, at the mouth of Globe and fountain Creek, encamped at night on its north side. Renewing their march next morning, they came, at the distance of six miles on the waters of Rutherford's Creek, near where Solomon Herring has since lived, upon the camp of the Indians. It was fired upon, when the Indians immediately fled, leaving one of their number dead. Captain Rains, with his company, then returned to Nashville.

The same vigilant officer soon after received the orders of Col. Robertson to raise another company, and scour the woods southwardly from Nashville, and destroy any Indians that might be found, east of the line dividing the Cherokee and Chickasaw nations. Sixty men constituted the command. They took the Chickasaw trace, crossing Duck River and Swan Creek, pursuing the Chickasaw path, which was recognized as the boundary. They then left the path, going south and east up the Tennessee River. After two days they came upon an Indian trail, and made pursuit. They overtook them, killed four men, and captured a boy. Seven horses, guns, blankets, skins, and all the Indians had, were taken The troop then returned to Nashville.

The boy, who had been taken prisoner in this engagement, was the son of a Chickasaw woman. His father was a Creek warrior. Mountain Leader, a distinguished chief of her nation, wrote, in behalf of the mother, to Capt. Rains, and proposed to exchange, for his prisoner, the son of a Mrs. Naine, who had been stolen by the Creeks from her, on White's Creek, and taken to the interior of their nation. Batterboo, a son of the Mountain Leader, had re-captured him from the Creeks. The exchange, as proposed, was agreed to and made.

In September, of this year, Captain Rains, being reinforced by a like number of men, commanded by Capt. Shannon, made his third expedition. The troop passed Green's Lick and Pond Spring, towards the head of Elk, scouring the woods in various directions. They came upon a fresh Indian trail, which they followed, and soon overtook the enemy. Capt. Rains, and one of his men, Beverly Ridley, pursued one of them and killed him. John Rains, Jr., and Robert Evans, outran another, and made him prisoner. All the rest escaped by flight. In the camp of this party were found large quantities of skins, and other plunder, which, with fifteen horses, fell into the hands of the whites.

Besides these excursions of Capt. Rains, other companies made similar expeditions in every direction throughout the country. Of the troops sent over Cumberland Mountain, to protect the infant settlements, was a company of rangers, commanded by Capt. William Martin. He remained in that frontier nearly two years; sometimes stationed in a fort, sometimes pursuing marauding parties of Indians, sometimes opening up channels of travel, by which emigrants could more easily reach the forming settlements.* The Indians soon became more wary in their invasions of the settlements, as the woods through which they had to pass were constantly traversed by armed bodies of men, endeavoring to find their trails and prevent their inroads. In addition to these companies raised from the settlers, a part of Major Evans's battalion was distributed over the country, and placed at the different stations, in such proportions as emergencies required. The command of Capt. Hadley remained for nearly two years, and added alike to the population and security of the country. Scouts were sent out from Bledsoe's Lick to the Cany Fork, under the command of Col. Winchester. They frequently fell upon Indian trails, and met war

---
*At the Talladega battle, after Col. Pillow was wounded, his Lieutenant-Colonel William Martin, took command, and was conspicuous for his good conduct.

parties in the woods, with great variety of fortune, sometimes disastrous and sometimes successful.

But, not withstanding all these measures of defence and precaution, the Indians occasionally succeeded in penetrating to the more exposed frontier stations, and murdering the inhabitants. In this way Samuel Buchanan was killed. The Indians came upon him, ploughing in the field, and fired upon him. He ran, and was pursued by twelve Indians, taking, in their pursuit, the form of a half-moon. When he came to the bluff of the creek, below the field, he jumped down a steep bank into the creek, where he was overtaken, killed and scalped. But the frontier, generally, was so vigilantly guarded by brave men, experienced in Indian fighting, that little success followed the incursions of the enemy—now more unfrequent, and conducted with timidity and caution.

[1788] The settlements had received considerable addition of emigrants. Agricultural pursuits were rewarded by bountiful crops, and the implacable enmity of the savages was the only interruption to general prosperity. In February, the Indians came to Bledsoe's Station, in the night time, and wounded George Hamilton, and went off. Near Asher's Station, on the north side of Cumberland, they wounded Jesse Maxey; he fell, and they scalped him and stuck a knife into his body. Contrary to expectation, he recovered.

The Indians came to the house of Wm. Montgomery, on Drake's Creek, in daylight, and killed, at the spring, not a hundred yards from the house, his three sons. In March, of the same year, a party of Creeks killed Peyton, the son of Col. James Robertson, at his plantation on Richland Creek, and captured a lad John Johnston, and retained him in captivity several years. Robert Jones was killed, some time afterwards, at Wilson's Station, and Benjamin Williams, near the head of Station-Camp Creek. Mrs. Neely was killed, and Robert Edmondson wounded, in Neely's Bend, and in October following, Dunham and Astill were killed.

These repeated acts of hostility on the part of the Creek nation, were generally ascribed to Spanish influence. That tribe had no real cause of displeasure against the people of Cumberland. They claimed no territory upon which settlements had been formed; no encroachments upon their possessions had been made; no acts of offensive war been perpetrated by Robertson and his colonists, except in defence of themselves and their families. Under these circumstances, it was determined to inquire, in a formal manner, from the Chief of the Creek nation, what were the grounds of their offensive deportment towards the settlers. Col. Robertson and Col. Anthony Bledsoe, therefore, addressed a joint letter to the celebrated McGillevray, which was transmitted to him by special messengers, Mr. Hoggatt and Mr. Ewing. To this communication, the chief replied from Little Tallassee, April 4, 1788. In his reply, he mentioned that, in common with other southern tribes, the Creeks had adhered to the British interest during the late war. That after peace was made, he had accepted proposals for friendship between their people, but that while that accommodation was pending, six of his nation were killed in the affair at Coldwater; and these warriors belonging to different towns, in each of which they had connexions of the first consequence, a violent clamour followed, which had given rise to the expeditions that afterwards took place against Cumberland. The affair at Coldwater, he continued, has since been amply retaliated, and I will now use my best endeavors to bring about a peace between us. This friendly overture was scarcely received on Cumberland, when, on the 20th of July, hostilities were again renewed.

Unfortunately for the country, the first victim was an individual prominent for his private virtues and for his public services, civil and military, rendered to the people on the frontier from the first settlement of Holston and Cumberland. Col. Anthony Bledsoe, having broken up his own fort, on what was known as the Greenfield Grant, had moved into the fort of his brother, Isaac Bledsoe, at Bledsoe's Lick, and occupied one end of his house. About midnight, of

July 20th, after the families living in the fort had retired to bed, James Clendening announced that the Indians were approaching near the houses. A party of them had formed an ambuscade about forty yards in front of the passage separating the houses of the brothers, and, with the view of drawing out the inmates, a few of the Indians rode rapidly through a lane near the fort. Col. Anthony Bledsoe, hearing the alarm, immediately arose, and, with his servant, Campbell, went boldly into the passage. The night was clear and the moon shone brightly. The Indians fired; Campbell was killed, and the Colonel received a mortal wound, being shot directly through the body. He died at sunrise next morning.

The fire of the Indians aroused William Hall, who was also at Bledsoe's Lick, and he made immediate preparation to resist a further anticipated attack. With some other gunmen, he went to the port-holes, and there remained till daylight. The Indians, seeing the fort was upon its guard, made no further assault, and withdrew.

At this period, it will be recollected, that the Union was in disorder, and on the point of dissolution from the imbecility of its own structure, and that North Carolina betrayed both inability and disinclination to furnish her trans-montane counties any assistance. Col. Robertson adopted the policy of temporizing and amusing, for the time being, both the Creek chieftain and the agents of Spain, and to dissemble the deep resentment their conduct had excited. With this view, he replied to McGillevray on the 3d of August, and though the recent death of his friend Col. Bledsoe, must have greatly irritated him, he suppressed every feeling of resentment and asperity. He acknowledged the satisfaction McGillevray's letter had given to his countrymen, and even seemed to extenuate the recent aggressions of the Creeks upon the settlers. He mentioned, without comment, the death of Col. Bledsoe, and as a means of further conciliation, added, that he had caused a deed for a lot in Nashville to be recorded in his name, and begged he would accept a tract or two of land in our young country. "I would say much to you," he continued, "respecting this fine country, but am fully sensible you are better able to judge what may take place a few years hence, than myself. In all probability, we cannot long remain in our present state, and if the British or any commercial nation, who may possess the mouth of the Misssssippi River, would furnish us with trade, and receive our produce, there cannot be a doubt, but that the people west of the Apalachian Mountains will open their eyes to their true interests. I shall be very happy to have your sentiments on these matters." This piece of diplomacy was not, as will be seen hereafter, without its effect upon those for whose use it was specially intended.

Thus skilfully did the young diplomatists at the Bluff, conduct the negotiation for its safety. To a further complaint made by McGillevray, of encroachments by settlers upon Creek territory, Col. Robertson again replied: "He regretted the circumstances, and excused both himself and the people of Cumberland from blame, by remarking, that they were not a part of the State* whose people made the encroachments. The people of Cumberland, he avowed, only claimed the lands which the Cherokees had sold in 1775, to Col. Henderson, and for which they were paid. He had not expected to be blamed for his late expedition, against the Indians below the Muscle Shoals, who were known to be a lawless banditti, and subject to the regulations of no nation. He had been subjected, recently, to the mortification of seeing one of his own children inhumanly massacred, a shock that almost conquered the fortitude which he had been endeavoring, from his earliest youth, to provide as a shield against the calamitous evils of this life. At the same time a neighbor's child was made prisoner, he requested the good offices of McGillevray to have restored. He had, last fall, stopped an excursion against the Cherokees, on hearing from Dr. White their friendly professions. He importuned McGillevray to punish the refratory part of his nation, as the only means of preserving peace." Here grief imper-

---
*Alluding to Franklin.

ceptibly stole upon his mind, and poured forth itself in nature's simple strains. "It is a matter of no reflection," said he, "to a brave man, to see a father, a son, or a brother, fall in the field of action. But it is a serious and melancholy incident to see a helpless woman or an innocent child tomahawked in their own houses."

To these strong and pathetic appeals of Col. Robertson, McGillevray replied, that he had endeavored to get the Little Turkey and Bloody Fellow to refrain future hostilities against the whites, and that he would persist in measures most proper to keep the Creeks from further hostilities against Cumberland.

The people of Tennessee have reason to venerate the memory of James Robertson, alike for his military and civil services, and the earnest and successful manner in which he conducted his negotiations for peace and commerce. His probity and weight of character, secured to his remonstrances with Indian and Spanish agents, respectful attention and consideration. His earnest and truthful manner was rarely disregarded by either.

[1788.] One hundred men, raised in Davidson and Sumner, and commanded by Col. Mansco and Major Kirkpatrick, escorted twenty-two families, who came this year by the way of the future Knoxville to Cumberland. These guards, to escort emigrant families through the wilderness, were continued several years, and afforded them almost perfect security from Indian disturbance. But wherever a house or a station was allowed to remain defenceless, murder and depredation followed. The Indians, after they killed Bledsoe, murdered one Walters, near Winchester's Mill. They attacked the station of Southerland Mayfield, upon the head of the west fork of Mill Creek, four miles above its junction with the east fork. The party consisted of ten or twelve Creek warriors. In the evening, they came to a place near the station where Mayfield, his two sons, Col. Jocelyn, and another person, were making a wolf pen. The Indians, unperceived, got between them and their guns. They fired upon and killed Mayfield, one of his sons, and another person, a guard at that station. They fired upon the guard and the son, as they went in the direction of the guns to bring to the pen something that was there, and jumped over a log, from where they had lain behind it, to scalp them, in the presence of Mayfield and Jocelyn. The latter ran for his gun and got amongst Indians, who fired upon him and drove him back, pursuing him in the form of a half moon. At length they drove him to a very large log, over which, if he could not have jumped, he was completely penned. Beyond his own expectation, Jocelyn leaped over the log and fell upon his back. Despairing of overtaking a man of so much activity, the Indians desisted from any further pursuit and left him. By a circuitous route he reached the station. Mayfield was wounded. He was not seen or pursued by the Indians, but was found next day dead. George Mayfield was taken prisoner, and held in captivity many years. Satisfied with the guns and the prisoner they had taken, the Indians made no assault upon the station, but made a hasty retreat. The people in the station then removed to Captain Rains, near Nashville. A mile below Mayfield's, the Indians attacked Brown's Station, and killed four boys—two of the sons of Stowball, one a son of Joseph Denton and the other a son of John Brown. Not long after, at the same station, James Haggard and his wife, John Haggard, and a man named Adams, were all killed. The people in this station then removed to Captain Rains.

On the 20th January, of this year, the Indians killed Capt. Hunter, and dangerously wounded Hugh F. Bell. A party of white men pursued, and, at the distance of two and a half miles, came upon them ambuscaded. They fired upon their pursuers, killed Major Kirkpatrick, and wounded J. Foster and William Brown. At Dunham's Station, in the spring, they killed —— Mills; in May, Dunham; and, in the summer, Joseph Norrington, and another Dunham, near the place where Joseph Irvin's house has since been built. J. Cockrill was fired at and his horse was killed. Besides these already mentioned, there were several others killed, whose names are not recollected. Hostilities continued throughout the summer, and Miss —— McGaughy, at Hickman's Station, and Hugh Webb, on the Kentucky trace, near Barren River, were killed by the Indians. Henry Ramsey was shot through the body, near Bledsoe's Creek, between Greenfield and Morgan's Station, three or four miles from Bledsoe's Lick.

[1789.] In May, Judge McNairy, with several others, on their way from Cumberland to what was then called *the settlements*, encamped for the night in the wilderness west of Clinch River. Next morning a large company of Indians fell upon them, killing one white man named Stanley, a Chickasaw chief called Longhair, and his son. The whites were entirely routed, and escaped only by swimming across the river. They lost all their horses, and the most of their clothing.

In June, the Indians made a bold attack on Robertson's Station. It was made in the day time, while the hands were at work in the field. In their escape to the fort, Gen. Robertson was wounded. He gave orders to Col. Elijah Robertson to send a force immediately against the Indians who had retreated. To Captain Sampson Williams was this service assigned, who, with sixty or seventy men, convened at Gen. Robertson's, marched at once, pursuing the enemy along McCutchin's trace, up West Harper, to the Ridge of Duck River. Here they discovered that the Indians out-travelled them. Twenty men were ordered to the front, to leave their horses, and to make forced marches upon the trail. Captain Williams and the twenty men, one of whom was Andrew Jackson, pushed forward and soon came in view of the Indian camp, on the south side of Duck River. They then went up the river a mile and a half, crossed over it in the night, and went down its bank to the place the Indian camp was supposed to be. The cane was so thick that they could not find the camp, and they lay on their arms all night. In the morning, Captain Williams advancing about fifty yards, descried the Indians repairing their fires, at the distance of one hundred yards from him. He and his men rushed towards them, fired at sixty yards distance, killed one, wounded five or six, and drove the whole party across the river to the north side. The Indians carried off their wounded and escaped, not taking time even to return the fire. In their flight they left to the victors sixteen guns, nineteen shot-pouches, and all their baggage, consisting of blankets, moccasins and leggins. They were not again overtaken. Near the mouth of the Sulphur Fork of Red River, the Indians fell upon the families of Isaac and John Titsworth, moving to the country. They, their wives and children, were all killed.

Evan Shelby, Abednego Lewellen, Hugh F. Bell, and Col. Tenen, were in the woods hunting. The two former were killed; the two last escaped.

In September, the Indians came to Buchanan's Station. John Blackburn, standing on the bank of the creek near the spring, was fired upon by ten or twelve of them at the same time He was killed, scalped, and left with a spear sticking in his body.

Among other emigrants from North Carolina to Cumberland, was the father of Col. William Pillow. He came through the wilderness with the guard commanded by Captain Elijah Robertson, and settled four miles south of Nashville, at Brown's Station. The son, William Pillow, was in most of the expeditions carried on against the Indians, from the time of his arrival in the country to the close of the Indian war. He was under Capt. Rains in the tour to Elk River, already mentioned. He also accompanied Captain John Gordon in pursuit of the Indians who had killed a woman near Buchanan's Station. Only one of the savages was killed; the rest effected their escape in the cane, and at night. He was also one of Captain Murray's company, who gave pursuit to the Indians, who, in February, killed John Helin at Jonathan Robertson's Station, six or seven miles below Nashville, and had also stolen several horses in that neighborhood. Murray's company crossed Duck River, five miles below the place where Columbia now stands, and continued a rapid march, day and night. The smoke from the enemy's camp was discovered, and four or five spies were sent forward. Capt. Murray charged obliquely to the right of the camp, which was on the bank of Tennessee River. His left charged obliquely to the left, and struck the river above the Indian camp. The spies fired and killed one; the other Indians ran down the river into Capt. Murray's line, when, finding their flight intercepted in that direction, they jumped into the river, and were shot. Mr. Maclin shot one before he got into the water. William Pillow, hearing a gun fire at a place which he had just passed, pushed his horse up the steep second river bank, and discovered Davis running towards him, pursued by four Indians. Pillow dashed forward, and the Indians, discontinuing the pursuit of Davis, ran off in the opposite direction. Pillow, pressing the pursuit too eagerly, fell from his horse; but recovered, sprang to his feet, gained upon the Indian, and discharged the contents of his musket into his body. At that moment, Capt. Murray, Thomas Cox, Robert Evans, Luke Anderson and William Ewing rode up, and Pillow pointed out to them the direction one of the Indians had gone. They immediately gave pursuit, and saw the Indian attempting to mount Pillow's horse, which he succeeded in doing. Cox ran up and shot him through the shoulder. The Indian, nevertheless, held on to

Pillow's horse, and kept him in a gallop till the whole company came up with him. He now slipped off the horse, and, as he came to the ground, scared Anderson's mule, which run under a low tree, whose limbs caught his gun and jerked it out of his hand. The brave Indian caught it up, snapped it three or four times at them, before Evans shot him down. Pursuit was then made by Andrew Castleman and others, after the two other Indians whom Pillow had driven from Davis. They were found hid in the water, under a bluff of rocks; both were killed. Others were found concealing themselves under the bank, and suffered the same fate. Eleven warriors were killed; the whole party, as was ascertained from the squaws who were taken prisoners.*

Such were the accumulated difficulties from savage hostility, undergone by the Cumberland settlements, in the first nine years after the arrival of Robertson at the Bluff. The p.ophecy of the sagacious Cherokee chief had been already fulfilled to the letter, and, still later, received further and stronger realization. "Much trouble" attended each step in the growth of the gallant community, of which the French Lick was the nucleus. And it may be safely said, that as the co-pioneers and compatriots of Robertson underwent trials, hardships, dangers, invasion, assault, massacre

---
*Manuscript Narratives.

and death from Indian warfare, unsurpassed, in degree and duration, in the history of any people; so they were endured with a fortitude, borne with a perseverance, encountered with a determination, resisted with a courage, and signalized with a valor, unequaled and unrecorded. The Bluff, the stations in its environs, the forts in its adjoining neighbourhoods, each hunting excursion, the settlement of each farm around the flourishing metropolis of Tennessee, furnishes its tale of desperate adventure and romantic heroism, upon which this writer dare not here linger.

"AN ACT FOR THE PROMOTION OF LEARNING IN THE COUNTY OF WASHINGTON."

Under the provision of this act the foundation of Martin Academy was laid. It is believed that this is the earliest legislative action taken anywhere west of the Alleghenies for the encouragement of learning. Jonesborough, State of Franklin, March 1st, 1785.

The first child born in the country was John Saunders, afterwards sheriff of Montgomery County, killed on White River by the Indians. The second born was Anna Wells. The first child born in Nashville was the son of Capt. Robertson---the late venerable relict of another age----Dr. Felix Robertson.

The Legislature also established a town at the Bluff. It was named Nashville, in honor of Col. Francis

Nash. He was an early advocate for resistance against arbitrary power—being a captain in the *Regulation* war in 1771, and appointed as early as the 24th of August, 1775, by the Congress of North Carolina, as one of a committee to prepare a plan for the regulation, internal peace, order and safety of the province. To this important committee was entrusted the duty of proposing a system of government, which would supply the want of an executive officer, arising from the absence of Governor Martin, who had fled from his palace, and of submitting other subordinate plans of government, such as the institution of Committees of Safety, the qualifications of electors, "and every other civil power necessary to be formed, in order to relieve the province in the present unhappy state to which the administration had reduced it."

September 1st, 1775, the North Carolina Congress appointed Mr. Nash, Lieutenant Colonel of the first regiment in the Continental service. At the battle of Germantown he commanded as Brigadier General, and at the head of his brigade, fell bravely fighting for the Independence of his country. Davidson and Nash were from the same State—bore the same rank in her armies—both fell in engagements that were unsuccessful to the American arms, but their names will be gratefully remembered, while the metropolitan county, and the metropolis itself of Tennessee, shall continue.

It is tradition, that the beautiful name given to our State in the Convention at Knoxville, in 1796, was suggested by General Jackson. The members from the *County* Tennessee consented to the loss of that name, if it should be transferred to the whole *State*. Its principal river still retained its aboriginal name, and the Convention adopted it, in preference to others that were spoken of. In euphony and smoothness, it compares well with those of her sister coterminous States, Alabama, Mississippi, Arkansas, Missouri and Kentucky; and, at the same time, is more American, less European, than her venerable mother, Carolina, or Virginia and Georgia.

The Congress of the United States passed an act in June, 1796, admitting Tennessee into the Union.

General James Robertson, this founder of the settlements on Watauga and Cumberland, this most successful negotiator between his countrymen and their Indian neighbors; this citizen, who so well united the character of the patriot and the patriarch, continued to the close of his useful life, an active friend of his country, and possessed in an eminent degree, the confidence, esteem and veneration of all his contemporaries; and his memory and services of the Western settlements, in peace and in war, are recollected with grateful regard by the present generation. He died a little earlier than his compatriot and colleague, Sevier. This event took place at the Chickasaw Agency, Sept. 1, 1814. (According to Ramsey.) Nashville was made the Capital of Tennessee in 1842. The Legislature met in Nashville, from 1812 to 1815, when it was transferred to Murfreesboro. Since 1826 that body has convened at Nashville, which became, by act of 1842, the permanent capital. From 1794 to 1812, the Territorial Legislature, met often at Knoxville.

We have thus traced the stream of emigration from the Atlantic to the West. We have seen a few enterprising and adventurous men, clustering together on the banks of the remote and secluded Watauga, felling the forest, erecting the cabin, forming society, and laying the foundation of government. We have seen the plain and unpretending emigrant from the Yadkin, and his hunter associates, combining the wisdom and virtue of the pioneer condition, and providing laws and regulations suited to the wants of the new community around them. We have seen the patriotism and chivalry of the extreme western settlement, rally at the sound of danger. Leaving their own frontier exposed, they magnanimously returned to the defence of a sister colony, and on the rugged Kenhawa, met and repulsed the savage invader. We have seen Robertson negotiate an enlargement of his borders, and effect a peaceable extension of the setments. We have seen the fortress erected, the station built, and the enemy repulsed. We have seen armaments by land and water boldly penetrate to the centre of the warlike Cherokee nation, and the soldiery of the Watauga bivouac upon the sources of the Coosa. The first settlement in Tennessee planted, defended, secure and prosperous, we have seen its founder and patriarch lead forth a new colony, through another wilderness, to experience upon another theatre, new privations, and undergo new dangers, and perform new achievements upon the remote Cumberland. There we will leave them.

In the eastern settlements was the cradle of the great State of Tennessee, where its infancy was spent and its early manhood formed. The vigorous shoots sent out from the parent stem—the colonies that have gone abroad from the old homestead, and peopled the great West—have ever been worthy of their ancestry. Their rapid growth and enlargement, their unexampled prosperity and achievement, are noticed with feelings of parental fondness and pride. In no spirit of servile arrogance is the claim upon their filia piety asserted for veneration and regard to their Forefathers. Through them our proud State claims to be one of the "Old Thirteen," and to be identified with them in the cause of Independence and Freedom.
(*Ramsey, Annals of Tennessee.*)

www.ingramcontent.com/pod-product-compliance
Lightning Source LLC
Chambersburg PA
CBHW030313170426
43202CB00009B/989